Jātaka

Folk Tales of the Buddha's Past Lives

Volume One

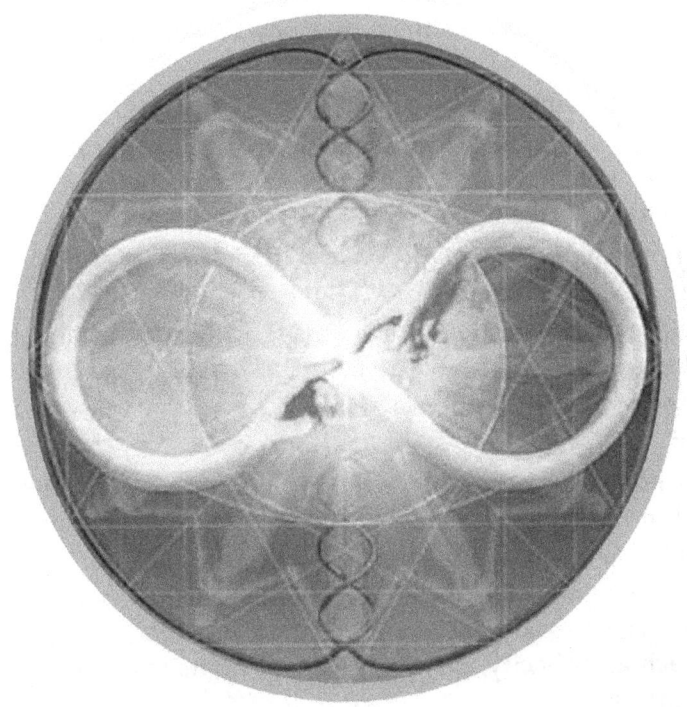

As told and illustrated by Eric K. Van Horn

originally translated by Robert Chalmers, B.A., of Oriel College, Oxford University

originally edited by Professor Edward Byles Cowell, Cambridge University

Copyright

You are free to:

Share - copy and redistribute the material in any medium or format

Adapt - remix, transform, and build upon the material

The licensor cannot revoke these freedoms as long as you follow the license terms.

Under the following terms:

Attribution - You must give appropriate credit and indicate if changes were made. You may do so in any reasonable manner, but not in any way that suggests the licensor endorses you or your use.

NonCommercial - You may not use the material for commercial purposes.

No additional restrictions - You may not apply legal terms or technological measures that legally restrict others from doing anything the license permits.

Notices:

You do not have to comply with the license for elements of the material in the public domain or where your use is permitted by an applicable exception or limitation.

No warranties are given. The license may not give you all of the permissions necessary for your intended use. For example, other rights such as publicity, privacy, or moral rights may limit how you use the material.

CreateSpace Independent Publishing Platform
ISBN-13: 978-1719063456
ISBN-10: 1719063451
First Edition 2018

*Dedicated to my children,
Without whom I might never have discovered
this wonderful literature.*

Other books by this author:

The Travel Guide to the Buddha's Path

The Little Books on Buddhism series:

Book 1: *The Little Book of Buddhist Meditation: Establishing a daily meditation practice*

Book 2: *The Little Book on Buddhist Virtue: The Buddha's teachings on happiness through skillful conduct*

Book 3: *The Little Book of the Life of the Buddha*

Book 4: *The Little Book of Buddhist Wisdom: The Buddha's teachings on the Four Noble Truths, the three marks of existence, causality, and karma*

Book 5: *The Little Book of Buddhist Mindfulness & Concentration*

Book 6: *The Little Book of Buddhist Daily Living: The Discipline for Lay People*

Book 7: *The Little Book of Buddhist Rebirth*

Book 8: *The Little Book of Buddhist Awakening: The Buddha's instructions on attaining enlightenment*

Table of Contents

Introduction 1
1: Apaṇṇaka Jātaka, *The True Dharma* 4
2: Vaṇṇupatha Jātaka *The Sandy Road* 14
3: Serivaṇija Jātaka, *The Gold Bowl* 19
4: Cullaka-seṭṭi Jātaka, *Chullaka the Treasurer* 23
5: Taṇḍulanāli Jātaka, *The Measure of Rice* 34
6: Devadhamma Jātaka, *Divine Virtue* 38
7: Kaṭṭahāri Jātaka, *Prince No-father* 44
8: Gāmani Jātaka, *Prince Gāmani* 48
9: Makhādeva Jātaka, *King Makhādeva* 51
10: Sukhavihāri Jātaka, *Dwelling in Happiness* 54
11: Lakkhaṇa Jātaka, *The Honorable Man* 59
12: Nigrodhamiga Jātaka, *Keep Only with the Banyan Deer* 63
13: Kaṇḍina Jātaka, *The Mountain Buck* 72
14: Vātamiga Jātaka, *The Greedy Antelope* 75
15: Kharādiyā Jātaka, *Kharādiyā's Story* 79
16: Tipallattha-miga Jātaka, *The Cunning Deer* 82
17: Māluta Jātaka, *In Light or Dark* 87
18: Matakabhatta Jātaka, *The Goat That Laughed and Cried* ... 89
19: Āyācitabhatta Jātaka, *On Offerings Given* 93
20: Naḷapāna Jātaka, *The Monkey King and the Ogre* 95
21: Kuruṅga Jātaka, *The Clever Antelope* 98
22: Kukkura Jātaka, *The Dog's Teaching* 101
23: Bhojājānīya Jātaka, *The War Horse* 106
24: Ājañña Jātaka, *The Thoroughbred War Horse* 110
25: Tittha Jātaka, *The Horse at the Ford* 112
26: Mahilāmukha Jātaka, *The Elephant Damsel-face* 117

27: Abiṇha Jātaka, *The Elephant and the Dog* 122
28: Nandivisāla Jātaka, *The Bull Who Won the Bet* 125
29: Kaṇha Jātaka, *The Old Woman's Black Bull* 128
30: Muṇika Jātaka, *The Ox Who Envied the Pig* 132
31: Kulāvaka Jātaka, *On Mercy to Animals* 135
32: Nacca Jātaka, *The Animals Choose Kings* 145
33: Sammodamāna Jātaka, *The Quarrel of the Quails* 148
34: Maccha Jātaka, *The Slave of Passion* 151
35: Vaṭṭaka Jātaka, *The Act of Truth* 154
36: Sakuṇa Jātaka, *The Unsuitable Tree* 158
37: Tittira Jātaka, *The Harmonious Friends* 161
38: Baka Jātaka, *The Crane and the Crab* 166
39: Nanda Jātaka, *Nanda and the Buried Gold* 171
40: Khadiraṅgāra Jātaka, *The Pit of Coals* 175
41: Losaka Jātaka, *The Story of Losaka* 186
42: Kapota Jātaka, *The Greedy Crow* 195
43: Veḷuka Jātaka, *Bamboo's Father* 199
44: Makasa Jātaka, *The Mosquito* 202
45: Rohiṇī Jātaka, *Rohiṇi's Tale* 205
46: Ārāmadūsaka Jātaka, *The Garden Spoiler* 208
47: Vāruṇi Jātaka, *The Liquor Spoiler* 211
48: Vedabbha Jātaka, *The Treasure Spell* 214
49: Nakkatta Jātaka, *The Stars* 219
50: Dummedha Jātaka, *The Evildoers* 223

Abbreviations for Pāli Text References

AN: *Aṅguttara Nikāya, The Numerical Discourses of the Buddha*
Bv: *Buddhavaṃsa, Chronicle of Buddhas*
BvA: *Buddhavaṃsatthakathā*, commentary to the *Buddhavaṃsa*
Cv: *Cullavagga*, the "smaller book," the second volume in the *Khandhaka*, which is the second book of the monastic code (the *Vinaya*)
Dhp: *Dhammapada, The Path of Dhamma*, a collection of 423 verses
DhpA: *Dhammapada-aṭṭhakathā*, commentary to the *Dhammapada*
DN: *Dīgha Nikāya, The Long Discourses of the Buddha*
Iti: *Itivuttaka, This Was Said* (by the Buddha), Sayings of the Buddha
Ja: *Jātaka Tales*, previous life stories of the Buddha
JaA: *Jātaka-aṭṭhakathā*, commentary on the *Jātaka Tales*
Khp: *Khuddakapāṭha, Short Passages*
MA: *Majjhima Nikāya Aṭṭhakathā*, commentary on *The Middle Length Discourses of the Buddha* (by Buddhaghosa)
MN: *Majjhima Nikāya, The Middle Length Discourses of the Buddha*
Mv: *Mahāvagga*, the first volume in the *Khandhaka*, which is the second book of the monastic code (the *Vinaya*)
Pm: *Pātimokkha, The Code of Monastic Discipline*, the first book of the monastic code (the *Vinaya*)
SN: *Saṃyutta Nikāya, The Connected Discourses of the Buddha*
S Nip: *Sutta Nipāta, The Sutta Collection*, literally, "suttas falling down," a sutta collection in the *Khuddaka Nikāya* consisting mostly of verse
Sv: *Sutta-vibhaṅga: Classification of the Suttas*, the "origin stories" for the Pātimokkha rules
Thag: *Theragāthā: Verses of the Elder Monks*
ThagA: *Theragāthā-aṭṭhakathā*: commentary to the *Theragāthā*
Thig: *Therīgāthā: Verses of the Elder Nuns*
ThigA: *Therīgāthā-aṭṭhakathā*: commentary to the *Therīgāthā*
Ud: *Udana, Exclamations*, the third book of the *Khuddaka Nikāya*
Vin: *Vinaya Pitaka, Basket of Discipline*, the monastic rules for monks and nuns.

Introduction

The Jātaka Tales are the Buddhist equivalent of Aesop's Fables. Coincidentally they date to about the same time, around the 5th century BCE. They are morality stories. Most of them are associated with one of the *pāramīs* (Pāli) or *pāramitās* (Sanskrit), the *Ten Perfections*. According to the Buddhist tradition, the Ten Perfections are qualities that the Buddha, in his previous lives as a *Bodhisatta* (Pāli, Sanskrit: *Bodhisattva*), cultivated in order to become the Buddha. The Ten Perfections are 1) generosity, 2) virtue, 3) renunciation, 4) wisdom, 5) effort, 6) patience, 7) honesty, 8) determination, 9) loving-kindness, and 10) equanimity.

(This formulation of the Ten Perfections is from Theravada, or Southern Buddhism. In Mahayana Buddhism there are Six Perfections: 1) generosity, 2) morality, 3) patience, 4) effort, 5) meditation, and 6) wisdom. The Buddha never referred to these qualities as the Ten/Six Perfections, although he often talked about these qualities. The categorization of these qualities as a distinct group probably came later.)

For many centuries and right up to the present day most lay Buddhists learned about the teachings of the Buddha from these stories. Lay people did not typically meditate or study the discourses, but they did learn the Jātaka Tales. As with Aesop's Fables, in these stories the Bodhisatta can be a person, a king, or an animal.

Some people object to stories of this type on the ground that they are not literally true. But as Joseph Campbell used to say, a myth is a metaphor. I can tell you about the importance of good judgment or wisdom, for example, but you are more likely to remember it if I tell you the charming story of Jātaka 54 in which a clever monkey outsmarts a crocodile.

The Jātaka Tales follow a formula in which there is a "story in the present" followed by the Jātaka Tale, which is then followed by the end of the story in the present. The story in the present gives the context in which the Buddha supposedly told it.

I am always warning people when it comes to literature of this type not to get too hung up on its literal truth. The Buddha taught a path to freedom from suffering. It is a path that ends in the greatest joy:

> *Any sensual bliss in the world,*
>   *any heavenly bliss,*
> *isn't worth one sixteenth-sixteenth*
> *of the bliss of the ending of craving.*
> - [Ud 2.2]

So I suggest that a more skillful way to read these stories is to concentrate on the lessons they teach and to take them to heart. These stories are quite charming and often playful, and no one ever said that the Buddha's path could not be fun.

As for the sources of these texts, the only complete translation of the Jātaka Tales is from the Pāli Text Society (PTS). They were originally published in six volumes between 1895 and 1907. The importance of the Pāli Text Society in Western Buddhist history cannot be overstated. PTS was founded in 1881 by Thomas William (T.W.) Rhys Davids and his wife Caroline. This was after T.W. published the first Pāli to English dictionary in 1874. At that time Buddhism in Sri Lanka (then called *Ceylon*) was under pressure from Christian missionaries. The Pāli Text Society was part of an effort that helped to revive Buddhism in Sri Lanka and laid the groundwork for our ability to read Pāli texts in English today.

The Jātaka Tales were originally translated and edited by Edward Byles Cowell, a professor at Cambridge University, William Henry Denham Rouse, a linguistics scholar and teacher who was also at Cambridge, Henry Thomas Francis, and R.A Neil, a fellow at Pembroke College. To them we owe a great debt. Having said that, the PTS editions use a lot of antiquated Victorian language, idioms, and punctuation. This makes them rather inaccessible to a modern audience.

My main goal with this effort is to make these wonderful stories more accessible, more fun (that word again!). This is not a scholarly effort. I am not a scholar or a Pāli translator. I have simply taken the original texts and edited them for a modern audience. I have also added some illustrations.

You will sometimes run across single Jātaka Tales in print, and some of them are really wonderful. One of my favorites is *The Magic of Patience*, which was also one of my childrens' favorite books when they were young. I strongly encourage you to find such publications. But here I want to take the entire body of literature, all 547 stories, and

Introduction

re-tell and edit the stories as a complete collection. The Jātaka Tales are sort of the guilty pleasure (or, to be more Buddhist, a harmless pleasure) of Buddhism. I hope that you will enjoy the result.

Eric K. Van Horn
Rio Rancho, NM
18-Dec-2017

1: Apaṇṇaka Jātaka,
The True Dharma

This is a story about wisdom. The Pāli word is "paññā" and the Sanskrit word is "prajñā." Ṭhānissaro Bhikkhu prefers to translate this as "discernment." It is not some thing that one obtains. It is an active quality, the ability to make good choices in the moment. Notice how in this story the wise merchant is able to observe the situation, analyze it, and make skillful decisions. Conversely, the foolish merchant is motivated by greed and ignorance.

In Buddhist practice, the Dharma provides the basis for making wise choices, and the practice of meditation develops the skill to see what is going on in the mind. The ability to develop this inner observer allows the practitioner to see defilements in the mind so that they do not inhibit good decision making. Likewise, the cultivation of good qualities supports the ability to make wise decisions.

The Blessed One told this story about the Dharma while he was staying in the Great Monastery at Jetavana near Sāvatthi. But what, you might ask, was it that led up to this tale?

It was 500 friends of the Buddha's great lay disciple Anāthapiṇḍika. They were followers of other religious leaders.

One day Anāthapiṇḍika took his 500 friends to Jetavana, and he also brought garlands, perfumes, and ointments, together with oil, honey, molasses, cloths, and cloaks. After paying homage to the Blessed One, he gave his gifts to the Saṅgha and sat down to the side. Likewise, the disciples of other schools saluted the Buddha and took their seats close by the side of Anāthapiṇḍika. They gazed upon the Master's countenance, glorious as the full moon, upon his excellent presence endowed with the signs and marks of Buddhahood and surrounded to a height of six feet with light, and upon the rich glory that marks a Buddha, a glory that issued as it were in paired garlands, pair upon pair.

Then, in the thunderous tones of a young lion roaring in the Red Valley, or as of a storm cloud in the rainy season, bringing down as it were the Ganges of the Heavens (i.e. the *Milky Way*) and seeming to weave a garland of jewels, yet in a voice of perfection, the charm of

1: Apaṇṇaka Jātaka,
The True Dharma

which ravished the ear, he preached to them the Dharma in a discourse full of sweetness and bright with varied beauty.

After hearing the Master's discourse, they rose up with hearts converted, and with due salutation to the Lord of Knowledge, they renounced the other doctrines in which they had taken refuge and went to the Buddha as their refuge. After that they always went to the monastery with Anāthapiṇḍika, carrying in their hands perfumes and garlands and the like, to hear the Dharma. They gave generously, kept the Five Precepts, and kept the weekly fast-day.

Subsequently the Blessed One left Sāvatthi and went back to Rājagaha. As soon as the Buddha left, they renounced their new faith, returned to the other doctrines, and reverted to their original state.

After he had been in Rājagaha for seven or eight months, the Blessed One went back to Jetavana. Once again Anāthapiṇḍika came with his friends to the Master, saluted him, offered perfumes and the like, and took his seat on one side. The friends also saluted the Blessed One and took their seats. Then Anāthapiṇḍika told the Blessed One how, after the Buddha left on his alms-pilgrimage, his friends had forsaken their refuge for the old doctrines and had reverted to their original state.

Opening the lotus of his mouth as though it were a casket of jewels scented with divine perfumes, the Blessed One made his sweet voice come forth as he asked, "Is it true that you, disciples, have forsaken the Three Refuges (i.e., *the Buddha, Dharma and Saṅgha*, also *the Three Gems*) for the refuge of other doctrines?"

Unable to conceal the truth, they confessed, saying, "It is true, Blessed One." Then the Master said, "Disciples, not between the bounds of hell below and the highest heaven above, not in all the infinite worlds that stretch right and left is there the equal, much less the superior, of the great rewards that spring from following the Five Precepts and from other virtuous conduct."

Then he declared the excellence of the Three Gems as they are revealed in the sacred texts. "Of all creatures, no matter what their form, of these the Buddha is the chief." Then he went on to say, "No disciples, male or female, who seek refuge in the Three Gems, that are endowed with such peerless excellences, are ever reborn into hell and other painful states. Released from all rebirth into states of suffering, they pass to the Realm of Devas and there they receive great glory.

Therefore, in forsaking such a refuge for that offered by other doctrines, you have gone astray."

But the Master did not end his teaching at this point. He went on to say, "Disciples, meditation on the thought of the Buddha, meditation on the thought of the Dharma, meditation on the thought of the Saṅgha gives entry to and fruition of the First, the Second, the Third, and the Fourth Paths to Bliss." (i.e. the four stages of awakening: *stream-entry, once return, non-return, and arahant.*) And when he had preached the Dharma to them in these and other ways, he said, "In forsaking such a refuge as this, you have gone astray."

When he had exhorted the disciples, the Blessed One said, "So too in times past, disciples, the people who jumped to the conclusion that what was no refuge was a real refuge, fell prey to goblins in a demon-haunted wilderness and were utterly destroyed, while the people who adhered to the absolute and indisputable truth, prospered in the same wilderness." And when he had said this, he became silent.

Then, rising up from his seat and saluting the Blessed One, Anāthapiṇḍika burst into praises. With clasped hands raised in reverence to his forehead, he said, "It is clear to us, sir, that in these present days these disciples were led by error into forsaking the supreme refuge. But the bygone destruction of those opinionated ones in the demon-haunted wilderness and the prospering of the men who adhered to the truth, are hidden from us and known only to you. May it please the Blessed One, as though causing the full moon to rise in the sky, to tell us the story of what happened."

Then the Blessed One said, "It was only by brushing away the world's difficulties and practicing the Ten Perfections (*generosity, virtue, renunciation, wisdom, effort, patience, honesty, determination, loving-kindness, and equanimity*) through many eons that I became a Buddha. Now listen as closely as if you were pouring pure liquid gold into a fine mold."

Having excited Anāthapiṇḍika's attention, he made clear the thing that rebirth had concealed from them, as though he were releasing the full moon from the upper air, the birthplace of the snows.

Once upon a time in the city of Benares in the Kāsi country there was a king named Brahmadatta. In those days, the Bodhisatta (*Buddha in a*

1: Apaṇṇaka Jātaka,
The True Dharma

previous life) was born into a merchant's family. When he grew up, he used to journey about trading with 500 carts, travelling first from east to west and then from west to east. There was also another young merchant at Benares, and he was very foolish.

Now at the time of our story, the Bodhisatta had loaded 500 carts with valuable merchandise from Benares and had them ready to depart. The foolish young merchant had done so as well. The Bodhisatta thought, "If this foolish young merchant travels with me and the 1,000 carts travel along together, it will be too much for the road. It will be very hard to get wood, water, and food for the men or grass for the oxen. Either he must go first, or I must go first."

So he went to the other merchant and said, "The two of us can't travel together. Would you rather go first or last?" The foolish merchant thought, "There will be many advantages if I go first. I will have a road that is not yet cut up. My oxen will have the pick of the grass. My men will have the pick of the herbs for curry. The water will be undisturbed. And lastly, I shall fix my own price for selling my goods." So he replied, "I will go first, my dear sir."

The Bodhisatta saw many advantages in going last. He thought, "Whoever goes first will level the road where it is rough, while I will travel along the road they have already travelled. Their oxen will have grazed off the coarse old grass, while mine will eat the sweet young growth that will spring up in its place. My men will find a fresh growth of sweet herbs for curry where the old ones have been picked. Where there is no water, the first caravan will have to dig to supply themselves, and we will drink at the wells they dug. Finally, haggling over prices is hard work, whereas I will sell my merchandise at the prices they have already fixed." Seeing all these advantages, he said to the other merchant, "Then you go first, my dear sir."

"Very well, I will," said the foolish merchant, and he yoked his carts and set out. Traveling along, he left human habitations behind him and came to the outskirts of the wilderness. Now there are five kinds of wildernesses: robber wildernesses, wild beast wildernesses, drought wildernesses, demon wildernesses, and famine wildernesses. The first is when the way is beset by robbers. The second is when the way is beset by lions and other wild beasts. The third is when there is no bathing or water to be got. The fourth is when the road is beset by demons. And the fifth is when no food is to be found. The wilderness in this case was both a drought wilderness and a demon wilderness.

The young merchant took great big water jars on his carts, and he set out to cross the ninety miles of desert that lay before him. When he reached the middle of the wilderness, the goblin who haunted it said to himself, "I will make these men throw away their water, and then I will kill them all when they are weak and we will eat them." So he used his magic power to make a beautiful carriage drawn by pure white young bulls appear. With some ten or twelve goblins bearing bows and quivers, swords and shields, he rode along to meet them like a mighty lord in this carriage. He had blue lotuses and white water lilies wreathed round his head, and he had wet hair and wet clothes. His carriage wheels were wet and muddy. His attendants, too, in front and rear of him went along with their hair and clothes wet, with garlands of blue lotuses and white water lilies on their heads, and with bunches of white lotuses in their hands. They chewed tasty stalks that were dripping with water.

At that time, it was the custom for caravan leaders to ride in front in their carriage with their attendants around them whenever the wind blew in their face. This was so they could escape the dust. But when the wind blew from behind them, they rode in the rear of the column. On this occasion, the wind was blowing against them, so the young merchant was riding in front.

When the goblin saw the merchant approach, he drew his carriage to the side of the road and greeted him kindly and asked him where he was going. Likewise, the merchant of the caravan drew his carriage to the side of the road to let the other carts pass by while he stayed behind to talk to the goblin. "We are just on our way from Benares, sir," he said. "But I see that you have lotuses and water lilies on your heads and in your hands, and that your people are chewing tasty stalks, and that you are all muddy and dripping with water. Did it rain while you were on the road, and did you come on pools covered with lotuses and water lilies?"

The goblin exclaimed, "What did you say? Why, just over there is a dark green forest, and after that there is nothing but water all through the forest. It is always raining there. The pools are full and there are lakes covered with lotuses and water lilies."

1: Apaṇṇaka Jātaka,
The True Dharma

Then as the line of carts passed by, he asked where they were going. The young merchant told him.

"And what goods do you have in your carts?"

The young merchant told him.

"And what do you have in this last cart? It seems to move as if it has a heavy load."

"Oh, there's water in that."

"You did well to carry water with you from the other side. But there is no need for it now. Water is abundant up ahead. You can break the jars and throw the water away. You won't need them and you will travel more easily." Then he added, "Now continue on your way. We have stopped here too long already." Then he went a little way further on until he was out of sight, and then he made his way back to the goblin city where he lived.

Figure: The Goblin and the Foolish Merchant

As you can probably guess, that foolish merchant did exactly as the goblin said. He broke his water jars and threw away all of his water. He did not save even enough to fit in the palm of your hand. Then he ordered the carts to drive on.

And of course, he did not find a drop of water. The men became exhausted from thirst. All day long they kept moving until the sun went down. At sunset they unyoked their carts and made camp, tying the oxen to the wheels. The oxen had no water to drink, and the men had none with which to cook their rice. The tired out band sank to the ground to sleep. But as soon as night fell, the goblins came out from their city and killed every single one of those men and oxen. And when they had eaten their flesh, leaving only the bare bones, the goblins left. Thus the foolish young merchant was the sole cause of the destruction of that entire caravan. Their skeletons were strewn in every conceivable direction, while the 500 carts stood there with their loads untouched.

Now the Bodhisatta allowed six weeks to pass before he set out. He left the city with his 500 carts, and in due course came to the outskirts of the wilderness. Here he had his water jars filled, and he laid in an ample stock of water. He assembled his men in camp and said, "Let not so much as a handful of water be used without my approval. There are poison trees in this wilderness, so no one should eat any leaf, flower, or fruit that he has not eaten before without first asking me." He then went into the wilderness with his 500 carts. When he reached the middle of the wilderness, the goblin showed up again. But, as soon as he became aware of the goblin, the Bodhisatta saw through him. He thought to himself, "There's no water here in this 'Waterless Desert.' This person with his red eyes and aggressive bearing casts no shadow. He has probably talked the foolish young merchant into throwing away all his water. Then he waited until they were worn out and killed the merchant and his men. But he doesn't know my cleverness and intelligence." He shouted to the goblin, "Be gone! We're men of business, and we do not throw away what water we have got before we see where more is to come from. But, when we do see more, we will throw this water away and lighten our carts."

The goblin rode on a bit further until he was out of sight, and then he went back to his home in the demon city. But when the goblin had gone, the Bodhisatta's men said to him, "Sir, we heard from those men that over there is the dark green forest where they said it was always raining. They had lotuses on their heads and water lilies in their hands and were eating tasty wet stalks. Their clothes and hair were wringing wet. Water was streaming off of them. Let us throw away our water and get on a more quickly with lightened carts."

1: Apaṇṇaka Jātaka,
The True Dharma

On hearing this the Bodhisatta ordered a halt and gathered all the men. "Tell me," he said, "Did anyone among you ever hear before today that there was a lake or a pool in this wilderness?"

"No, sir," they answered. "It's known as 'the Waterless Desert.'"

"We have just been told by some people that it is raining just on ahead, in the belt of forest. Now how far does a rain-wind carry?"

"Three or four miles, sir."

"And has this rain-wind reached any one man here?"

"No, sir."

"How far off can you see the crest of a storm cloud?"

"Three or four miles, sir."

"And has any one man here seen the top of even a single storm cloud?"

"No, sir."

"How far off can you see a flash of lightning?"

"Twelve or fifteen miles, sir."

"And has any one man here seen a flash of lightning?"

"No, sir."

"How far off can a man hear a peal of thunder?"

"About six to ten miles, sir."

"And has any man here heard a peal of thunder?"

"No, sir."

"These are not men but goblins. They will return in the hope of attacking us when we are weak and faint after throwing away our water. As the young merchant who went on before us was not a wise man, most likely he was fooled into throwing away his water and was killed when they were exhausted. We may expect to find his 500 carts standing just as they were loaded for the start. We will come on them today. Continue on with all possible speed without throwing away a drop of water."

Urging his men forward with these words, he proceeded on his way until he came upon the 500 carts standing just as they had been loaded.

The skeletons of the men and oxen were strewn about in every direction. He had his carts unyoked and arranged in a circle to form a fortified camp. He saw that his men and oxen had their supper early, and that the oxen were made to lie down in the middle with the men around them. He himself along with the leading men of his band stood guard, swords in hand through the three watches of the night, waiting for the day to dawn.

The next day at daybreak, after he had fed the oxen and all the necessary preparations were done, he discarded his own weak carts for stronger ones. He exchanged his own common goods for the most valuable of the abandoned goods. Then he went on to his destination where he bartered his stock for wares of two or three times their value. He came back to his own city without losing a single man out of all his company.

The story having ended, the Master said, "Thus it was, layman, that in past times the foolish came to utter destruction, while those who stuck to the truth escaped from the demons' hands. They reached their goal in safety and came back to their homes again." And having linked the two stories together, the Buddha spoke the following stanza for the purposes of this lesson on the Dharma:

> *Then some declared the only, the peerless Dharma,*
> *But otherwise the false prophet spoke.*
> *Let a person who is wise learn from this lesson,*
> *And firmly grasp the only, the peerless Dharma.*

Thus did the Blessed One teach this lesson about respecting the Dharma. And he went on to say, "What is called 'walking in truth' not only bestows the three happy endowments, the six heavens of the realms of sense, and the endowments of the higher Realm of Brahma, it finally leads to Arahatship. While what is called 'walking in untruth' entails rebirth in the four states of punishment or in the lowest classes of mankind."

Further, the Master went on to expound in sixteen ways the Four Truths (i.e. *The Four Noble Truths*) at the close of which all those 500 disciples were established in the Fruit of the First Path (*stream-entry*).

Having delivered his lesson and his teaching, and having told the two stories and established the connection linking them together, the

1: Apaṇṇaka Jātaka,
The True Dharma

Master concluded by identifying the story as follows, "Devadatta was the foolish young merchant. of those days. His followers were the followers of that merchant. The followers of the Buddha were the followers of the wise merchant, who was myself."

(Devadatta was a monk and the Buddha's cousin. He conspired to take over the Saṅgha and even tried to kill the Buddha.)

2: Vaṇṇupatha Jātaka
The Sandy Road

This is a story about perseverance, persistence, and determination. The Pāli word is "Adhiṭṭhāna" and in Sanskrit it is "Adhiṣṭhāna." In the Theravada formulation it is the eighth of the Ten Perfections.

Anyone who has practiced for even a short time can probably relate to the frustration of the poor monk who was unable to make any progress during his retreat. Ṭhānissaro Bhikkhu once said that when he went back and looked at the talks given by his teacher Ajahn Lee, the majority of them were words of encouragement. Being able to be both patient and relentlessly persistent are instrumental parts of the Buddha's path.

"Untiring, deep they dug." This discourse was delivered by the Blessed One while he was dwelling at Sāvatthi.

About whom, you ask?

About a monk who gave up persevering.

Tradition says that, while the Buddha was dwelling at Sāvatthi, an heir from a wealthy Sāvatthi family came to Jetavana. When he heard a discourse by the Buddha, he realized that craving leads to suffering, and he was admitted to the Saṅgha as a novice monk. After five years passed in preparing for full ordination, the Buddha gave him a theme for meditation that was appropriate for him. Retiring to a forest, he spent the rainy season there, but for all his striving during the three months, he was unable to make any progress. So he thought, "The Master said there were four types of men, and I must belong to the lowest of all. In this birth, I do not think that there is either path nor fruit for me. What good will it do for me to live in the forest? I will go back to the Master and live my life beholding the glories of the Buddha's presence and listening to his sweet teachings." And back he went to Jetavana.

Now his friends and intimates said, "Sir, it was you who obtained a theme of meditation from the Master and departed to live the solitary life of a sage. Yet here you are back again, going about enjoying fellowship. Can it be that you have attained awakening and that you will never know rebirth?"

2: Vaṇṇupatha Jātaka
The Sandy Road

"Sirs, as I won neither path nor fruit, I felt myself doomed to futility, and so gave up persevering and came back."

"You have done wrong, sir, in showing weakness when you had devoted yourself to the doctrine of the dauntless Master. Come, let us bring you to the Buddha." And they took him with them to the Master.

When the Master became aware of their coming, he said, "Monks, you bring this brother against his will. What has he done?"

"Sir, after devoting himself to so absolutely true a doctrine, this brother has given up persevering in the solitary life of a sage and has come back."

Then the Master said to him, "Is it true, as they say, that you, brother, have given up persevering?"

"It is true, Blessed One."

"But how is it that after devoting yourself to such a doctrine, that you should not prove to be someone who desires little, who is contented, solitary, and determined, but someone who lacks perseverance? Especially because you were so stout-hearted in the past. Was it not you who single-handedly saved the men and oxen in a caravan of 500 carts in a sandy desert thanks to your perseverance, and that because of that you were cheered? And how is it that, now, you are giving in?" These words sufficed to give heart to that monk.

Hearing this talk, the other monks asked the Blessed One, saying, "Sir, the present weakness of this brother is clear to us. But tell us how this single man was able to get water for the men and oxen in a sandy desert and was cheered. This is known only to you. Please tell us about it."

"Listen O monks," said the Blessed One. And, having excited their attention, he made clear the thing that rebirth had concealed from them.

Once upon a time when Brahmadatta was King in Benares in Kāsi, the Bodhisatta was born into a trader's family. When he had grown up, he used to travel about trading with 500 carts. On one occasion, he came to a sandy wilderness over 200 miles across. The sand was so fine that when you squeezed it in your hand, it slipped through the fingers of even a tightly closed fist. As soon as the sun came up, it got as hot as a bed of charcoal embers, and nobody could walk upon it. Accordingly, those traveling across it used to take firewood, water, oil, rice, and so forth on their carts, and only traveled by night. At dawn they used to arrange their carts in a circle to form a camp with an awning spread overhead, and after an early meal used to sit in the shade all day long. When the sun went down, they had their evening meal. Only when the ground became cool would they yoke their carts and move forward. Traveling on this desert was like voyaging over the sea. A "desert-pilot," as he was called, had to convoy them over by knowledge of the stars. And this was the way in which our merchant was now traveling that wilderness.

When he had only some seven more miles before him, he thought to himself, "Tonight will see us out of this sandy wilderness." So, after they had had their supper, he ordered the wood and water to be thrown away, and yoking his carts, set out on the road. The pilot sat in the front cart on a bench looking up to the stars in the heavens and directing their course. But he was so tired that he fell asleep, and as a result he did not see that the oxen had turned around and were retracing their steps. All night the oxen kept on their way, but at dawn the pilot woke up, and, observing the disposition of the stars overhead, shouted out, "Turn the carts round! Turn the carts round!"

As they turned the carts round and were forming them into line, the day broke. "Why this is where we camped yesterday," cried the people of the caravan. "All our wood and water are gone, and we are lost." So they unyoked their carts and made camp and spread the awning overhead. Then each man flung himself down in despair beneath his own cart. The Bodhisatta thought to himself, "If I give in, every single one will perish." So he walked back and forth while it was still early and cool until he came on a clump of kusa grass. "This grass," he thought, "can only have grown up here thanks to the presence of water underneath." So he ordered a shovel to be brought and a hole to be dug at that spot. They dug down very deep until they struck a rock, and everybody lost heart. But the Bodhisatta, feeling sure there must be water under that rock, went down in the hole and stood on the rock. Stooping down, he put his ear on it and listened. Catching the sound of water flowing beneath, he came out and said to a servant boy, "My boy, if you give in, we shall all perish. So take heart and have courage. Go down into the hole with this iron sledge hammer and strike the rock."

2: Vaṇṇupatha Jātaka
The Sandy Road

Figure: The Courageous Servant

Doing as the Bodhisatta asked, the lad, resolute where all others had lost heart, went down and struck the rock. The rock, which had dammed the stream, split apart and fell in. The water rose up in the hole until it was as high as a palm tree, and everybody drank and bathed. Then they chopped up their spare axles and yokes and other surplus gear, cooked their rice and ate it, and fed their oxen. As soon as the sun set, they hoisted a flag by the side of the well and traveled on to their destination. There they sold their goods for twice and four times their value. They returned to their own home with their profits where they lived out their lives, and in the end passed away to fare thereafter according to their karma. The Bodhisatta, too, after a life spent in charity and other good works, passed away likewise to fare according to his karma.

When the Supreme Buddha had delivered this discourse, he, the All-Knowing One himself, uttered this stanza:

> *Untiring, deep they dug that sandy track*
> *Till, in the trodden way, they found water.*
> *So let the sage, strong in perseverance,*
> *Flag not nor tire, until his heart finds peace.*

This discourse having ended, he preached the Four Noble Truths, at the close of which the fainthearted brother was established in the highest fruit of all, which is Arahatship.

Having told these two stories, the Master established the connection linking them both together, and identified the birth by saying: "This fainthearted brother of today was in those days the servant boy who persevered and broke the rock and gave water to all the people. The Buddha's followers were the rest of the people of the caravan, and I myself was their leader."

3: Serivaṇija Jātaka,
The Gold Bowl

This tale uses the same story in the present as Jataka 2 in which a monk loses heart, and it supposedly has the same themes of perseverance, persistence, and determination. However, it seems to me that this story is more about honesty and kindness on one hand and greed on the other. Read it and see what you think.

The origins of the Jātaka tales are not known, but many were probably borrowed and adapted to Buddhist themes from stories that already existed in India at the time of the Buddha. It is possible that since the story in the present was borrowed from Jātaka 2 that this is one of them. However it came to be a part of the Jātaka collection, it is a good story with a good theme.

"*If in this faith.*" This lesson, too, was taught by the Blessed One while at Sāvatthi, also about a monk who gave up persevering.

For, when the man was brought by the Saṅgha exactly as in the previous story, the Master said, "You, Brother, who after devoting yourself to this glorious doctrine which bestows path and fruit, are giving up persevering, will suffer long, like the merchant of Seri who lost a golden bowl worth a hundred thousand pieces."

The monks asked the Blessed One to explain this to them. The Blessed One made clear a thing concealed from them by rebirth.

Once upon a time in the kingdom of Seri, many years ago, the Bodhisatta dealt in pots and pans. Because his family name was "Serivan," they called him "the Serivan." There was also another merchant of that same name, and he was a very greedy person. He came from across the river Telavāha, and he entered the city of Andhapura. They agreed to divide the city between them, and so the first merchant set about hawking his wares in the streets of his district, and the other did the same in his district.

Now in that city there was a destitute family. Once they had been rich merchants, but by the time of our story they had lost all the sons and brothers and all their wealth. The sole survivors were a girl and her grandmother, and they made their living by working for hire. Nevertheless, they had a golden bowl in their house. In the old days the great merchant, the head of the family, used to eat from it. But it had been thrown among the pots and pans, and it was so dirty that the two women did not know that it was gold.

Now the greedy merchant came to the door of their house crying, "Water pots to sell! Water pots to sell!" And the young girl said to her grandmother, "Oh, do buy me a trinket, grandmother."

"We're very poor, dear. What can we offer in exchange for it?"

"Why here's this bowl which is no good to us. Let us change that for it."

The old woman invited the merchant in, and she gave him the bowl, saying, "Take this, sir, and be so good as to give my granddaughter something in exchange."

The merchant took the bowl in his hand and turned it over. Because he knew the weight and feel of gold, he suspected what the bowl was made of. He surreptitiously scratched a line on the back of it with a needle, and then he knew for certain that it was real gold. Then, thinking that he would get the pot without giving anything whatever for it to the women, he cried, "What's the value of this? Why it isn't worth anything!" And with that he threw the bowl on the ground, rose up from his seat, and left the house.

Now, the two merchants had agreed that the one might try the streets that the other had already been to. So the first merchant came into that same street and appeared at the door of the house, crying, "Water pots to sell!" Once again the young girl made the request of her grandmother, and the old woman replied, "My dear, the first merchant threw our bowl on the ground and ran out of the house. What have we got left to offer now?"

"Oh, but that merchant was a harsh man, grandmother dear, while this one looks a nice man and speaks kindly. Perhaps he would take it."

"Call him in then."

So he came into the house, and they gave him a seat and put the bowl into his hands. He immediately knew that the bowl was gold. He said, "Mother, this bowl is worth a hundred thousand pieces. I do not have that much money with me."

3: Serivaṇija Jātaka,
The Gold Bowl

"Sir, the first merchant who came here said that it was not worth anything, so he threw it to the ground and went away. It must have been because of your own goodness that the bowl turned into gold. Take it and give us something or other for it and then go your way."

At the time the merchant had 500 coins and a stock worth as much more. He gave all of this to them, saying, "Let me keep my scales, my bag, and eight pieces of money, and you can have the rest."

They agreed to this, and he departed as quickly as he could to the river where he gave his eight coins to a boatman and jumped into the boat. Subsequently that greedy merchant came back to the house, and he asked them to bring out their bowl. He said he would give them something or other for it. But the old woman raged at him with these words, "You said that our golden bowl, which is worth a hundred thousand pieces, was not worth anything. But there came an upright merchant who gave us a thousand pieces for it and took the bowl away."

Figure: The Greedy Merchant

He angrily exclaimed, "He has robbed me of a golden bowl worth a hundred thousand pieces. He has caused me a terrible loss!"

An intense anger came upon him, so that he lost control over himself. He threw his money and goods at the door of the house. He threw off his upper and under cloths, and, armed with the beam of his scales as a club, he tracked the good merchant down to the river. There he found that the good merchant had already started across the river. He shouted to the boatman to come back, but the good merchant told him not to do so. As the greedy merchant stood there gazing at the retreating honest merchant, intense anger seized him, His heart grew hot. Blood gushed from his lips, and his heart cracked like the mud at the bottom of a tank that the sun has dried up. Because of the intense hatred he had towards the good merchant, he died right then and there.

The good merchant, after a life spent in charity and other good works, passed away to fare according to his karma.

When the Supreme Buddha ended this lesson, he, the All-Knowing One himself, uttered this stanza:

> *If in this faith you prove remiss, and fail*
> *To win the goal where its teachings lead,*
> *Then, like the greedy merchant called "the Serivan,"*
> *Full long you'll regret the prize your folly lost.*

After delivering his discourse in such a way as to lead up to Arahatship, the Master expounded the Four Noble Truths, after which the fainthearted monk attained that highest fruit of all, which is Arahatship.

And after telling the two stories, the Master made the connection linking them both together and identified the birth by saying in conclusion, "In those days Devadatta was the greedy merchant, and I was the wise and good merchant." This was the first time Devadatta conceived a grudge against the Bodhisatta.

4: Cullaka-seṭṭi Jātaka,
Chullaka the Treasurer

There are many people who think that there is a stigma attached to making money, but you will not find that in the Buddha's teachings. He often praised people who were astute in business. Of course, he also made it clear that business must be honest and fair, but there is nothing negative attached to earning a good living. The Buddha also gave advice on how money should be responsibly managed, to account for calamities, to take care of your family, and to support charitable causes.

In this story a clever young man is able to start with nothing but a humble mouse and turn it into a fortune.

"*With humblest start.*" The Master told this story while he was staying at Jīvaka's Mango grove near Rājagaha. (*Jīvaka was King Bimbisāra's court physician and a prominent lay disciple of the Buddha's.*) It is about an elder monk named Little Wayman. And here we must preface the story by giving an account of Little Wayman's origins.

The daughter of a rich merchant's family in Rājagaha became romantically involved with a servant. She was afraid that her family would find out about their affair, so she said to the servant, "We can't stay here, for if my mother and father find out about us, they will tear us limb from limb. Let us go and live far away from here." So carrying everything they could, they snuck out of the house and ran away.

They eventually found a place to live, and after a while the daughter became pregnant. When it was nearly time for her to give birth, she said to her husband, "If I go into labor without being with my family, there will be trouble for us both. So let us go home." (*It was the custom in those days for a pregnant woman to go back to her family and give birth there.*) At first he agreed to leave right away, but then he put it off until the next day. He kept doing this day after day until she thought to herself, "This fool is so afraid of his offense that he dares not go. One's parents are one's best friends, so whether he goes or stays, I must go." So, when he went out, she put all her household matters in order and left, telling her next-door neighbor where she was going. When he returned home and did not find his wife, he found out from the neighbor that she had started off home. He hurried after her and caught up with her on the road, just after she had given birth.

"What's this, my dear?" he said.

"I have given birth to a son, my husband," she said.

Accordingly, as she had already given birth, they both agreed that there was no reason to go on, and so they turned back again. And as their child had been born by the way, they called him "Wayman."

Not long after, she became pregnant again, and everything happened as before. And as this second child too was born by the way, they also called him "Wayman," calling the older son "Big Wayman" and the younger son "Little Wayman" Then, with both their children, they again went back to their own home.

As he got older, Big Wayman heard other boys talking about their uncles and grandfathers and grandmothers. So he asked his mother if he had relatives like the other boys. "Oh yes, my dear," his mother said, "But they don't live here. Your grandfather is a wealthy merchant in the city of Rājagaha, and you have many relatives there."

"Why don't we go there, mother?" he said.

She told the boy why they stayed away. But as the children kept on asking about their relatives, she finally said to her husband, "The children are always pestering me. Are my parents going to eat us? Come, let us show the children their grandfather's family."

"Well, I don't mind taking them there, but I really could not face your parents."

"All right," she said. "As long as, some way or other, the children are able to see their grandfather's family."

So they took their children and went to Rājagaha. They stayed in a public rest house by the city gate. Then they sent word to her parents that they were in the city and wanted the children to see their grandparents and family. The latter, on hearing the message, returned this answer, "True, it is strange to be without children unless one has renounced the world and become a monk or a nun. Still, your offense is so great that we will not see you. However, here is some money for you. Take it and go live where you want. But you may send the children here."

Then the merchant's daughter took the money and sent the children back with the messengers. So the children grew up in their

4: Cullaka-seṭṭi Jātaka,
Chullaka the Treasurer

grandfather's house. Because he was older, Big Wayman used to go with his grandfather to hear the Buddha preach the Dharma. And by constantly hearing the Dharma from the Master's own lips, the boy's heart yearned to renounce the world for the life of a monk.

"With your permission," he said to his grandfather, "I would like to join the Sangha."

"What do I hear?" cried the old man. "Why, it would give me greater joy to see you join the Sangha than to see the whole world join. Become a monk, if you wish." And he took him to the Master.

"Well, merchant," said the Master, "Have you brought your boy with you?"

"Yes sir. This is my grandson, and he wants to join the Sangha." Then the Master sent for a senior monk and told him to admit the boy to the Sangha. The monk performed the ordination ceremony and admitted the boy as a novice monk. When the boy had memorized many discourses and was old enough, he was given the higher ordination as a full monk. He now devoted himself to the training until he won Arahatship.

As he passed his days in the enjoyment of insight and the path, he thought about imparting the same happiness to Little Wayman. So he went to his grandfather and said, "Great merchant, with your consent, I will admit Little Wayman to the Sangha."

"Please do so, reverend sir," his grandfather replied.

Then the elder admitted the boy Little Wayman and gave him the novice ordination. But Little Wayman proved a dullard. Even after studying for four months he was unable to learn even this single stanza:

> *Lo! like a fragrant lotus at the dawn*
> *Of day, full-blown, with virgin wealth of scent,*
> *Behold the Buddha's glory shining forth,*
> *As in the vaulted heaven beams the sun!*

Sadly, we are told that his brother ridiculed the dull Little Wayman. His scorn so hurt the novice monk that it was impossible for him to learn this passage. Each new line he learned drove the last one out of his memory, and as the four months slipped by, he was still struggling with this single stanza. His brother said to him, "Wayman, you do not deserve to receive this doctrine. In four whole months you have been unable to learn a single stanza. How can you hope to achieve supreme success? You should leave the monastery."

But, even though he was expelled, Little Wayman so loved the Buddha's teaching that he did not want to become a layman.

Now at that time Big Wayman was acting as steward. And Jīvaka Komārabhacca, going to his mango grove with a large present of perfumes and flowers for the Master, had presented his offering and listened to a discourse. Then, rising from his seat and bowing to the Buddha, he went up to Big Wayman and asked, "How many monks are there, reverend sir, with the Master?"

"Just 500, sir."

"Will you bring the 500 monks, with the Buddha at their head, to take their meal at my house tomorrow?"

"Lay disciple, one of them named Little Wayman is a dullard and makes no progress on the path," said the senior monk. "I accept the invitation for everyone but him."

Hearing this Little Wayman thought to himself, "In accepting the invitation for all these monks, my brother carefully accepts so as to exclude me. This proves that my brother's affection for me is dead. My situation here is hopeless. I will become a layman and exercise charity and the other good works of a lay person." And early the next day he left the monastery, intending to become a layman again.

Now at the first break of day, as he was surveying the world, the Master became aware of this, and leaving even earlier than Little Wayman, he waited on the road that he knew Little Wayman would take. As Little Wayman came up the road, he saw the Master, and with a salutation went up to him. The Master said, "Where are you going at this hour, Little Wayman?"

"My brother has expelled me from the Saṇgha, sir, and so I am leaving."

"Little Wayman, because you took your vows under me, why did you not come to me when your brother expelled you? What would you do with a layman's life? You shall come with me."

4: Cullaka-seṭṭi Jātaka,
Chullaka the Treasurer

He then took Little Wayman and seated him at the door of his own perfumed hut. He gave him a perfectly clean cloth which he had supernaturally created, and the Master said, "Face towards the east, and as you handle this cloth, repeat these words: 'Removal of impurity. Removal of impurity.'" Then at the time appointed, the Master, attended by the Saṅgha, went to Jīvaka's house and sat down on the seat set for him.

Now Little Wayman, with his gaze fixed on the sun, sat handling the cloth and repeating the words, "Removal of impurity. Removal of impurity." And as he kept handling the piece of cloth, it got increasingly dirty. Then he thought, "This piece of cloth was quite clean, but my personality has destroyed its purity and made it dirty. Indeed, all conditioned things are impermanent!" And just as he saw into the truth of death and decay, he attained the first stage of awakening, stream entry.

Knowing that Little Wayman's mind had awakened, the Master sent an apparition and an image of himself appeared before him, as if seated in front of him, and said, "Heed it not, Little Wayman, that this mere piece of cloth has become dirty and stained with impurity. Within you are the impurities of lust and other evil things. Remove *them*." And the apparition uttered these stanzas:

> *Lust is impurity, not dirt.*
> *We call lust the real impurity.*
> *Yea, monk, who drives it from his breast,*
> *He lives the gospel of the purified.*
>
> *Anger is impurity, not dirt.*
> *We call anger the real impurity.*
> *Yea, monk, who drives it from his breast,*
> *He lives the gospel of the purified.*
>
> *Ignorance is impurity, not dirt.*
> *We call ignorance the real impurity.*
> *Yea, monks, who drives it from his breast,*
> *He lives the gospel of the purified.*

At the close of these stanzas Little Wayman attained a full awakening, to Arahatship, with the four branches of knowledge (*(1) understanding the meaning of the Dharma, (2) understanding its ethical truth, (3) the ability to understand it logically, and (4) the ability to teach it*), whereby he came to know all the sacred teachings.

Tradition has it that in ages past, when he was a king and was making a solemn procession around his city, he wiped the sweat from his brow with a spotless cloth that he was wearing, and the cloth was stained. He thought, "It is this body of mine which has destroyed the original purity and whiteness of the cloth and dirtied it. All conditioned things are indeed impermanent." Thus he grasped the idea of impermanence, and subsequently it was the removal of impurity which achieved his salvation.

Meantime, Jīvaka Komārabhacca offered the Water of Donation (*When a gift was made, the donor poured water over the hand of the donee*), but the Master put his hand over the vessel, saying, "Are there any monks, Jīvaka, in the monastery?"

Big Wayman responded, "There are no monks there, reverend sir."

"Oh yes, there are, Jīvaka," said the Master.

"Hey, there!" said Jīvaka to a servant. "Go and see whether or not there are any monks in the monastery."

At that moment Little Wayman, aware that his brother was declaring there were no monks in the monastery, determined to show him there were. He used his newly acquired psychic powers to project a host of monks into the mango grove. Some were making robes, others dyeing, while others were chanting discourses. He made every monk different from all the others. When the servant saw so many monks at the monastery, he returned and said that the whole mango grove was full of monks.

But as regards the monk at the monastery:

> Wayman, a thousand-fold self-multiplied,
> Sat on, until bidden, in that pleasant grove.

"Now go back," said the Master to the servant," and say 'The Master sends for him whose name is Little Wayman.'"

But when the man went and delivered his message, a thousand mouths answered, "I am Little Wayman! I am Little Wayman!"

The man came back and reported, "They all say they are 'Little Wayman,' reverend sir."

4: Cullaka-seṭṭi Jātaka,
Chullaka the Treasurer

"Well now go back," said the Master, "and take the hand of the first one of them who says he is Little Wayman, and the others will all disappear." The man did as he was told, and immediately the thousand monks disappeared. Little Wayman came back with the servant.

When the meal was over, the Master said, "Jīvaka, take Little Wayman's bowl. He will return thanks." Jīvaka did so. Then, like a young lion roaring defiance, Little Wayman ranged the whole of the discourses through in his address of thanks. Finally, the Master rose from his seat and, attended by the Saṇgha, returned to the monastery. There, after the assignment of tasks by the Saṇgha, he rose from his seat and, standing in the doorway of his perfumed hut, delivered a discourse. He ended with a theme that he gave out for meditation, and dismissing the Saṇgha, he went into his perfumed hut and lay down lion-like on his right side to rest.

The yellow-robed monks assembled together from all sides in the hall and sang the Master's praises. It was said, "Big Wayman failed to see the capacity of Little Wayman and expelled him from the monastery as a dullard who could not even learn a single stanza in four whole months. But the All-Knowing Buddha by his supremacy in the Dharma bestowed on him Arahatship with all its supernatural knowledge, even while a meal was in progress. And by that knowledge he grasped the whole of the sacred texts. Oh! how great is a Buddha's power!"

Now the Blessed One, knowing full well the discussion that was going on in the Dharma Hall, thought it appropriate to go there. So he put on his two yellow under-robes, girded himself as with lightning, arrayed himself in his yellow outer robe, the ample robe of a Buddha, and went to the Dharma Hall with the infinite grace of a Buddha, moving with the royal gait of an elephant with an abundance of vigor. Ascending the glorious Buddha-throne set in the midst of the resplendent hall, he seated himself upon the middle of the throne emitting those six-colored rays which mark a Buddha, like the newly-arisen sun, when from the peaks of the Yugandhara Mountains he illumines the depths of the ocean. When the All-Knowing One came into the Hall, the monks broke off their talk and were silent. Gazing round on the company with gentle loving-kindness, the Master thought within himself, "This company is perfect! Not a man is guilty of moving hand or foot improperly. Not a sound, not a cough or sneeze is to he heard! In their reverence and awe of the majesty and glory of the Buddha, not a man would dare to speak before I did, even if I sat here in silence all my life long. But it is my part to begin, and I will open the conversation." Then in his sweet divine tones he addressed the monks and said, "What were you just talking about?"

"Sir," they said, "it was not idle chatter. We were praising you."

And when they had told him word for word what they had been saying, the Master said, "Monks, through me Little Wayman has just now risen to great things in the practice. In the past he also rose to great things as well. He became wealthy, also because of me."

The monks asked the Master to explain this, and the Blessed One made clear in these words a thing that had been hidden from them.

Once upon a time, when Brahmadatta was reigning in Benares in Kāsi, the Bodhisatta was born into the treasurer's family, and after growing up, became the treasurer himself. Thus he was called the "Little Treasurer." He was a wise and clever man, with a keen eye for signs and omens. One day on his way to wait upon the king, he came on a dead mouse lying on the road. Noticing the position of the stars at that moment, he said, "Any decent young fellow with his wits about him has only to pick that mouse up, and he might start a business and keep a wife."

Nearby there was a young man who was from a good family, but they had recently had some bad fortune. He heard what the Little Treasurer said, and thought, "That's a man who always has a good reason for what he says." And so he picked up the mouse, which he then sold for a small coin at a tavern for their cat.

With the small coin he bought some honey and got some drinking water in a water pot. He went out to find some flower gatherers who were returning from the forest. He gave each a tiny quantity of the honey and ladled the water out to them. Each of them gave him a handful of flowers. He sold the flowers and the next day, he came back again to the flower grounds with more honey and a pot of water. That day the flower gatherers, before they went, gave him flowering plants with half the flowers left on them, and thus, after selling them, he had eight coins.

4: Cullaka-seṭṭi Jātaka,
Chullaka the Treasurer

Later, one rainy and windy day, the wind blew down a quantity of rotten branches and boughs and leaves in the King's pleasure garden, and the gardener could not figure out how to clear them away. The young man offered to remove the debris, if he could keep the wood and leaves. The gardener immediately agreed. Then this apt pupil of the Little Treasurer went to the children's playground and bribed them with honey to collect every stick and leaf in the place into a heap at the entrance to the pleasure garden.

Figure. The Little Treasurer and the Mouse

Just then the king's potter was on the lookout for fuel to fire bowls for the palace, and coming on this heap, bought the lot off his hands. The sale of the wood brought in sixteen coins to this pupil of the Little Treasurer, as well as five bowls and other vessels.

He now had 24 coins in all, and then he had another idea. He went to the city gate with a jar full of water and supplied 500 mowers with water to drink. They said, "You've done us a kind favor, friend. What can we do for you?"

"Oh, I'll tell you when I want your help," he said.

As he wandered about, he struck up friendships with a land trader and a sea trader. The land trader said to him, "Tomorrow a horse dealer with 500 horses to sell will come to town."

On hearing this, he said to the mowers, "I want each of you today to give me a bundle of grass and not to sell your own grass until mine is sold."

"Certainly," they said and delivered the 500 bundles of grass at his house.

The next day, the horse dealer was, not surprisingly, unable to get grass for his horses elsewhere. So the horse dealer bought our friend's grass for a thousand coins.

Only a few days later his sea trading friend told him about the arrival of a large ship in port, and he had another idea. He hired a well-appointed carriage for eight coins and went in great style down to the port. He bought the ship on credit and deposited a signet ring as security. He had a pavilion built nearby and said to his people as he took his seat inside, "When merchants are being shown in, have them pass by three successive ushers into my presence." Hearing that a ship had arrived in port, about a hundred merchants came down to buy the cargo, only to be told that they could not have it as a great merchant had already bought everything. So they all went to the young man, and the footmen duly announced them by three successive ushers. Each man of the hundred gave him a thousand pieces to buy a share in the ship and then another thousand to buy him out altogether. So it was with 200,000 pieces that this pupil of the Little Treasurer returned to Benares.

To show his gratitude, he went with one hundred thousand pieces to call on the Little Treasurer. "How did you come by all this wealth?" asked the Treasurer. "In four short months, simply by following your advice," replied the young man, and he told him the whole story, starting with the dead mouse.

The Lord High Treasurer, on hearing all this, thought "I must see that this resourceful young fellow does not fall into anybody else's hands." So he married him to his own grown-up daughter and settled all the family estates on the young man. And at the Treasurer's death, the young man became treasurer in that city.

And the Little Treasurer passed away to fare according to his karma.

His lesson ended, the Supreme Buddha, the All-Knowing One himself, repeated this stanza:

With humblest start and trifling capital
A shrewd and able man will rise to wealth,
Even as his breath can nurse a tiny flame.

Also the Blessed One said, "It is through me, monks, that Little Wayman has just now risen to great things in the path, as in times past to great things in the way of wealth." His lesson thus finished, the Master made the connection between the two stories he had told and identified the birth in these concluding words, "Little Wayman was in those days the pupil of the Little Treasurer, and I myself was Lord High Treasurer."

5: Taṇḍulanāli Jātaka,
The Measure of Rice

I think this story may have been assembled long after the Buddha died. One reason that I think this is because in the story there is someone who is assigned to give rice to the monks. During the Buddha's time, this most probably would not have happened. The monks and nuns went on alms rounds unless it was the rainy season. This story feels like later Buddhism when it was more institutionalized. It also does not seem correct to me that elder monks would get a higher quality of rice than younger monks. During the Buddha's time alms food was usually gathered individually but then assembled and distributed evenly to the entire Saṅgha.

In addition, this story does not feel in the line of the Buddha's teaching and his character. The Buddha and the monks treats Udāyi quite harshly. Of course, the Buddha could be quite severe with his monks if they misbehaved. He was especially hard on monks who espoused wrong views. However, he hardly ever was harsh on anyone in other contexts. But read it for yourself and see what you think.

"*Do you ask how much a measure of rice is worth?*" This was told by the Master, while he was at Jetavana, about the Elder Udāyi, called the Dullard.

At that time the reverend Dabba, the Mallian, was the steward in charge of gathering and distributing provisions for the monastery. When Dabba allotted the portions for rice in the early morning, sometimes it was choice rice and sometimes it was an inferior quality. On these days the Elder Udāyi ended up getting the inferior rice. When that happened, Udāyi would make a fuss in the distribution room by demanding, "Is Dabba the only one who can give out rice? Can't *we* do that as well?"

One day when he was making a fuss, they handed him the rice basket and said, "Here! you give the rice out yourself today!" After that, it was Udāyi who gave out the rice to the monks.

But Udāyi could not tell the best from the inferior rice, and he did not know which monks were entitled to the best rice and which to the inferior. So too, when he was making out the roster (*the list of most senior to most junior monks*), he had no idea who were the most senior monks. Consequently, when the monks took up their places, he made

5: Taṇḍulanāli Jātaka,
The Measure of Rice

a mark on the ground or on the wall to show that senior monks stood here and junior monks there. Next day there were fewer monks of one grade and more of another in the distribution room. Where there were fewer, the mark was in the wrong place. Likewise, when there were more, it was also in the wrong place. But Udāyi, quite ignorant of the differences, gave out the portions according to his old marks.

So the monks said to him, "Friend Udāyi, the mark is in the wrong place. The best rice is for those who are senior, and the inferior quality for those who are junior." But he said back to them, "If this mark is where it is, what are you standing here for? Why should I believe you? I trust my mark."

Then the novices threw him out of the distribution room, crying, "Friend Udāyi the Dullard, when you give out the portions, the monks do not get their proper shares. You are not fit to give them out. Get out of here." And a great uproar arose in the room.

Hearing the noise, the Master asked the Elder Ānanda, "Ānanda, what is the noise all about?"

Ānanda explained what had happened to the Buddha. "Ānanda," he said, "This is not the only time that Udāyi has robbed others of their profit because of his stupidity. He did just the same thing in bygone times too."

Ānanda asked the Blessed One for an explanation, and the Blessed One made clear what had been concealed by rebirth.

Once upon a time Brahmadatta was reigning in Benares in Kāsi. In those days our Bodhisatta was his appraiser. He used to determine the value of horses, elephants, jewels, gold, and so on, and he used to pay the owners of the goods a fair price that he fixed.

But the King was greedy and he thought, "This appraiser with his style of valuing will soon exhaust all the riches in my house. I must get another appraiser." So he opened his window and looked out into his courtyard. There he saw a stupid, greedy ass of a man who he thought would be a good candidate for the post. So the King sent for the man and asked him whether he could do the work. "Oh yes," said the man. And so, to safeguard the royal treasure, this stupid fellow was appointed appraiser.

After this the fool, in appraising elephants and horses and the like, used to assign a price dictated by his whim, neglecting their true worth. But, because he was the appraiser, the price was what he said and could not be challenged.

At that time a horse-dealer with 500 horses arrived from the north country. The King sent for his new appraiser and told him to assign a value to the horses. The price he set on the 500 horses was just one measure of rice. He ordered this to be paid to the dealer and directed the horses to be led off to the stable. The horse-dealer then went to see the old appraiser. He told him what had happened and asked if there was anything that he could do to get a fair price. "Give him a bribe," said the ex-appraiser, "and say this to him: 'Now that you have determined that our horses are worth just a single measure of rice, we are curious to know the precise value of a measure of rice. Could you tell us its value in the presence of the King?' If he says that he can, then take him before the King, and I will be there, too."

Following the Bodhisatta's advice, the horse-dealer bribed the man and put the question to him. The appraiser, having expressed his ability to value a measure of rice, was promptly taken to the palace. The Bodhisatta and many other ministers went as well. With appropriate respect the horse-dealer said to the King, "Sire, I do not dispute that the value of 500 horses is a single measure of rice, but I would like to ask your majesty to ask your appraiser what is the value of that measure of rice."

Ignorant of what had happened, the King said to the fellow, "Appraiser, what are 500 horses worth?"

"A measure of rice, sire," he replied.

"Very good, my friend. If 500 horses then are worth one measure of rice, what is that measure of rice worth?"

"It is worth all Benares and its suburbs," was the fool's reply.

Thus we learn that, having first valued the horses at a measure of rice to please the King, he was bribed by the horse-dealer to estimate that measure of rice at the worth of all Benares and its suburbs. Yet the fool priced all this vast city and its suburbs at a single measure of rice!

The ministers clapped their hands and laughed uproariously. "We used to think," they said scornfully, "that the earth and the realm were

5: Taṇḍulanāli Jātaka, The Measure of Rice

priceless. But now we learn that the kingdom of Benares together with the King is only worth a single measure of rice! How talented the appraiser is! How has he kept his post so long? But truly the appraiser suits our King admirably."

Figure: A Really Terrible Appraiser!

Then the Bodhisatta repeated this stanza:

> *Do you ask how much a measure of rice is worth?*
> *Why, all Benares, both within and out.*
> *Yet, strange to tell, five hundred horses too*
> *Are worth precisely this same measure of rice!*

Thus put to shame, the King sent the fool packing, and gave the Bodhisatta the office again. And when his life closed, the Bodhisatta passed away to fare according to his karma.

His lesson ended and the two stories told, the Master made the connection linking both together, and identified the birth by saying in conclusion, "Udāyi the Dullard was the stupid rustic appraiser of those days, and I myself the wise appraiser."

6: Devadhamma Jātaka,
Divine Virtue

There are some lovely but understated moments in this story. There is the moment when the King kisses his elder sons before tearfully seeing them off. There is the selflessness of the youngest brother who decides to be loyal to his older brothers and go with them. And then there is the wisdom of the Bodhisatta, who not only saves his younger brothers, but saves the water-demon himself.

This is another case where the story-in-the-present is probably from a later time. It is hard to believe that any monk during the Buddha's time would have been able to provide for himself in the way that the misbehaving monk does.

"*Only those who are godlike call.*" This story was told by the Blessed One while at Jetavana, about a wealthy monk.

Tradition tells us that, on the death of his wife, a wealthy landowner from Sāvatthi joined the Saṅgha. When he joined, he had a chamber built for him with a room for a fire and a store-room. He did not formally join the Saṅgha until he stocked his store-room with ghee, rice, and the like. Even after he became a monk, he used to send for his servants and have them cook what he liked to eat. He was richly provided for. He had an entire change of clothing for night and another for day, and he lived separate from the rest of the monks on the outskirts of the monastery.

One day when he had taken out his cloths and bedding and had spread them out to dry in his chamber, a number of monks from the country, who were on a pilgrimage from monastery to monastery, came to his cell and found all these belongings.

"Whose are these?" they asked.

"Mine, sirs," he replied.

"What, sir?" they cried. "This upper-cloth and that as well, this under-cloth as well as that, and that bedding too, this is all yours?"

"Yes, nobody's but mine," he replied.

"Sir," said they, "the Blessed One has only sanctioned three robes, and even though the Buddha to which you have devoted yourself is so

6: Devadhamma Jātaka,
Divine Virtue

simple in his wants, you have all these possessions. Come! We must take you before the Lord of Wisdom." And, so saying, they took him to the Master.

Becoming aware of their presence, the Master said, "Why have you brought the monk against his will?"

"Sir, this monk is well-off and has quite a lot of possessions."

"Is it true, monk, as they say, that you are so well-off?"

"Yes, Blessed One."

"But why, monk, do you have so much? Don't you know that I praise wanting little, contentment, and so forth, solitude, and determined resolve?"

Angered by the Master's words, he cried, "Then I'll go about like this!" And, ripping off his outer clothing, he stood in their wearing nothing but his underwear.

Then with patience and compassion, the Master said, "Was it not you who in the past was ashamed to behave in an unwholesome, unworthy way? And even when you were a water-demon, you lived for twelve years in a virtuous way? How can it be that, after vowing to follow the Dharma, you have ripped off your outer robes and stand here devoid of shame?"

At the Master's word, his healthy sense of shame (*In the Buddha's teaching a healthy sense of shame is used as a deterrent to behaving unskillfully*.) was restored. He put on his robes again, and, saluting the Master, seated himself at the side.

The monks then asked the Blessed One to explain to them the story to which he referred, the Blessed One made clear what had been concealed from them by rebirth.

Once upon a time Brahmadatta was reigning in Benares in Kāsi. The Bodhisatta was born as the son of the King and the Queen, and he was named Prince Mahiṃsāsa. By the time he could run about, a second son was born to the King, and the name they gave this child was Prince Moon. But by the time he could run about, the Bodhisatta's mother died. Then the King took another Queen, who was his joy and delight, and their love was crowned with the birth of yet another prince, who they named Prince Sun. In his joy at the birth of the boy, the King promised to grant her any boon she might ask on the child's behalf. But the Queen asked that she be able to decide what she wanted at a later time. And once her son grew up, she said to the King, "Sire, when my boy was born, you granted me a boon to ask for him. Let him be King."

"No," said the King. "I have two older sons who are as radiant as flaming fires. I cannot give the kingdom to your son." But the queen kept pestering him to grant her request. And finally the King became afraid that she would harm his sons, so he sent for them and said, "My children, when Prince Sun was born, I granted a boon, and now his mother wants the kingdom for him. I have no wish to give him the kingdom, but I am afraid that she will conspire against you. You had better go off to the forest and only return after my death to rule in the city that belongs by right to our house." So with tears and lamentations, the King kissed his two sons on the head and sent them away.

As the princes were leaving the palace, Prince Sun, who had been playing in the courtyard, saw them. When he found out what had happened, he decided to go with his brothers. So he too went off in their company.

The three princes went to the Himalayas, and there the Bodhisatta sat down at the foot of a tree, and he said to Prince Sun, "Run down to the that pool over there. Drink and bathe there and then bring us back some water in a lotus-leaf."

That pool happened to have been given to a water-sprite by Vessavaṇa (*Vessavaṇa is another name for Kuvera, the Hindū Plutus, half-brother of Rāvaṇa, the demon-king of Ceylon in the Rāmāyaṇa. Vessavaṇa had rule over tree-sprites as well as water-sprites.*), who said to him, "With the exception of those who know what is truly godlike (*i.e., virtuous and wise*), you may devour anyone that goes down into this pool. But you only have power over those who go into the water." And after that the water-sprite used to ask all who went down into the pool what was truly godlike, devouring everyone who did not know.

Now quite unsuspecting Prince Sun went into this pool, and he was seized by the water-sprite who said to him, "Do you know what is truly godlike?"

6: Devadhamma Jātaka,
Divine Virtue

"Oh, yes," he said. "The sun and moon."

"You don't know," said the monster, and he hauled the prince down into the depths of the water and imprisoned him there. After Prince Sun had been gone for a long time, the Bodhisatta sent Prince Moon to see what had happened. He too was seized by the water-sprite and asked whether he knew what was truly godlike. "Oh yes, I know," he said. "The four quarters of heaven are."

"You don't know," said the water-sprite, and he hauled this second victim off to the same prison.

When he thought that his second brother had been gone too long, the Bodhisatta felt sure that something was wrong. So he went after them and traced their footsteps down into the water. He realized at once that the pool must be the domain of a water-sprite. He strapped on his sword, took his bow in his hand, and waited. Now when the demon figured out that the Bodhisatta had no intention of entering the water, he assumed the shape of a forester, and in this disguise said to the Bodhisatta, "You're tired from your journey, friend. Why don't you go in and have a bath and a drink, and cover yourself with lotuses? You will feel better afterwards."

But knowing that he was a demon, the Bodhisatta said, "It is you who have taken my brothers."

"Yes, it was," the water-sprite admitted.

"Why?"

"Because all who go down into this pool belong to me."

"What, all?"

"Except for those who know what is truly godlike, all who go into the water are mine."

"And do you want to know what is godlike?"

"I do."

"If this is true, then I will tell you what is truly godlike."

"Do so, and I will listen."

"I should like to begin," said the Bodhisatta, "but I am tired and dirty from my journey."

Then the water-sprite bathed the Bodhisatta and gave him food to eat and water to drink. He decked him with flowers, sprinkled him with scents, and laid out a couch for him in the midst of a gorgeous pavilion. Seating himself on this couch and making the water-sprite sit at his feet, the Bodhisatta said, "Listen then and you shall hear what the truly godlike is." And he repeated this stanza:

The godlike are those who shrink from doing harm,
The white-souled, tranquil, devoted disciples of good.

Figure: The Bodhisatta and the Water-demon

And when the demon heard this, he was pleased, and said to the Bodhisatta, "Man of wisdom, I am pleased with you, and I will give you back one of your brothers. Which one should I bring?"

"The youngest."

"Man of wisdom, though you know what the truly godlike is, you don't act from wisdom."

"How so?"

6: Devadhamma Jātaka,
Divine Virtue

"Why, you take the younger instead of the elder, without regard to his age."

"Demon, I not only know but practice the godlike. It was because of this boy that we sought refuge in the forest. His mother asked our father to give him the kingdom, but our father refused. As a result we had to run away to the refuge of the forest. This boy came with us of his own accord and never thought of turning back. No one would believe me if I told them that he had been devoured by a demon in the forest, and it is the fear of this backlash that compels me to ask for him."

"Excellent! excellent! Oh man of wisdom," cried the demon in approval. "You not only know but practice what is godlike." And in token of his pleasure and approval he brought back both brothers and gave them to the Bodhisatta.

Then the Bodhisatta said to the water-sprite, "Friend, it is because of your evil deeds in the past that you are now a demon living on the flesh and blood of other creatures, and in this life you continue to do evil. This evil conduct will keep you from escaping rebirth in hell and other evil states. From this time forward, you should renounce evil and live virtuously."

In this way the demon was converted from his evil ways. The Bodhisatta continued to live there under his protection, until one day he read in the stars that his father was dead. Then taking the water-sprite with him, he returned to Benares and took possession of the kingdom. He made Prince Moon his chief deputy and Prince Sun his commander-in-chief. He made a home for the water-sprite in a pleasant spot and made sure he was given the choicest garlands, flowers, and food. He himself ruled in righteousness until he passed away to fare according to his karma.

His lesson ended, the Master preached the Four Noble Truths, after which that monk won the Fruit of the First Path, stream-entry. And the All-knowing Buddha, having told the two stories, connected them together and identified the birth by saying, "The well-to-do monk was the water-demon of those days. Ānanda was Prince Sun, Sāriputta was Prince Moon, and I myself was the eldest brother, Prince Mahimsāsa."

7: Kaṭṭahāri Jātaka,
Prince No-father

Many Jātaka Tales have the theme of honesty. As Sarah Shaw points out in her book *"The Jātakas: Birth Stories of the Bodhisatta,"* in the Bodhisatta's many lives, he failed every virtuous quality except for honesty. For, as she says, *"a Bodhisatta might lapse in other ways but cannot say what is not true."*

"Your son am I." This story was told by the Master while at Jetavana about the story of Vāsabha Khattiyā, which will be found in the Bhaddasāla Jātaka (*Jātaka 74*).

Tradition tells us that she was the daughter of Mahānāma Sakka who in turn was the daughter of a slave girl named Nāgamuṇḍā, and that she afterwards became the consort of the King of Kosala.

She conceived a son by the King, but the King discovered that she was descended from a servant, and he revoked her privileges and status and also degraded her son Viḍūḍabha. The mother and son never went outside the palace.

When he heard about this, the Master went to the palace at early dawn attended by five hundred monks, and, sitting down on the seat prepared for him, said, "Sire, where is Vāsabha Khattiyā?"

Then the King told him what had happened.

"Sire, whose daughter is Vāsabha Khattiyā?"

"Mahānāma's daughter, sir."

"When she came away, to whom did she come as wife?"

"To me, sir."

"Sire, she is a king's daughter. She is married to a king, and to a king she bore her son. Why is that son not in authority over the realm? In bygone days, a monarch who had a son by a casual wood-gatherer gave his son his sovereignty."

The King asked the Blessed One to explain this. The Blessed One made clear what had been concealed from him by rebirth.

7: Kaṭṭahāri Jātaka,
Prince No-father

Once upon a time, the King of Benares went on a picnic in the forest. The beautiful flowers and trees and fruits made him very happy. As he was enjoying their beauty, he slowly went deeper and deeper into the forest. Before long, he became separated from his companions and realized that he was all alone.

Then he heard the sweet voice of a young woman. She was singing as she collected firewood. To keep from being afraid of being alone in the forest, the King followed the sound of the lovely voice. When he finally came upon the singer of the songs, he saw that she was a beautiful fair young woman and immediately fell in love with her. They became very friendly, and the King became the father of the firewood woman's child.

Later, he explained how he had gotten lost in the forest, and he convinced her that he was indeed the King of Benares. She gave him directions for getting back to his palace. The King gave her his valuable signet ring and said, "If you give birth to a baby girl, sell this ring and use the money to bring her up well. If our child turns out to be a baby boy, bring him to me along with this ring for recognition." So saying, he departed for Benares.

In the fullness of time, the firewood woman gave birth to a cute little baby boy. Being a simple shy woman, she was afraid to take him to the fancy court in Benares, but she saved the King's signet ring.

In a few years, the baby grew into a little boy. When he played with the other children in the village, they teased him and mistreated him, and even started fights with him. It was because his mother was not married that the other children picked on him. They yelled at him, "No-father! No-father! Your name should be No-father!"

Of course this made the little boy feel ashamed and hurt and sad. He often ran home crying to his mother. One day, he told her how the other children called him, "No-father! No-father! Your name should be No-father!" Then his mother said, "Don't be ashamed, my son. You are not just an ordinary little boy. Your father is the King of Benares!"

The little boy was very surprised. He asked his mother, "Do you have any proof of this?" So she told him about his father giving her the signet ring, and that if the baby was a boy she should bring him to Benares along with the ring as proof. The little boy said, "Let's go then." Because of what had happened, she agreed, and the next day they set out for Benares.

When they arrived at the King's palace, the gate keeper told the King the firewood woman and her little son wanted to see him. They went into the royal assembly hall, which was filled with the King's ministers and advisers. The woman reminded the King of their time together in the forest. Finally she said, "Your majesty, here is your son."

The King was ashamed in front of all the ladies and gentlemen of his court. So, even though he knew the woman spoke the truth, he said, "He is not my son!" Then the lovely young mother showed the signet ring as proof.

Again the King was ashamed and denied the truth, saying, "It is not my ring!"

Then the poor woman thought to herself, "I have no witness and no evidence to prove what I say. I have only my faith in the power of truth." So she said to the King, "If I throw this little boy up into the air, if he truly is your son, may he remain in the air without falling. If he is not your son, may he fall to the floor and die!"

Figure: Faith in the Power of Honesty

7: Kaṭṭahāri Jātaka,
Prince No-father

Suddenly, she grabbed the boy by his foot and threw him up into the air. Lo and behold, the boy sat in the cross-legged position, suspended in mid-air, without falling. Everyone was astonished, to say the least! Remaining in the air, the little boy spoke to the mighty King. "My lord, I am indeed a son born to you. You take care of many people who are not related to you. You even maintain countless elephants, horses and other animals. And yet, you do not think of looking after and raising me, your own son. Please do take care of me and my mother."

Hearing this, the King's pride was overcome. He was humbled by the truth of the little boy's powerful words. He held out his arms and said, "Come to me my son, and I will take good care of you."

Amazed by such a wonder, all the others in the court put out their arms. They too asked the floating little boy to come to them. But he went directly from mid-air into his father's arms. With his son seated on his lap, the King announced that he would be the crown prince, and his mother would be the number one queen.

In this way, the King and all his court learned the power of truth. Benares became known as a place of honest justice. In time the King died. The grownup crown prince wanted to show the people that all deserve respect, regardless of birth. So he had himself crowned under the official name, "King No-father!" He went on to rule the Kingdom in a generous and righteous way.

His lesson to the King of Kosala ended, and his two stories told, the Master made the connection linking them both together, and he identified the Birth by saying: "Mahāmāyā was the mother of those days, King Suddhodana was the father, and I myself King Kaṭṭhavāhana."

8: Gāmani Jātaka,
Prince Gāmani

This story is a little terse and requires some explanation. In the Pāli Text Society edition it says that the "Introductory Story and the Story of the Past will be given in the Eleventh Book with the Saṃvara Jātaka." This is Jātaka 462.

Jātaka 462 tells the story of a king with 100 sons. As each one of them comes of age, he is given a province over which to rule. However, when the youngest son comes of age, the Bodhisatta counsels him not to do this, but to stay behind and help his father rule. Over a period of years, with the Bodhisatta's advice he does this in a particularly humane and wise way. As a result he becomes very popular with people at all levels in the kingdom. When his father dies, despite the fact that he is the youngest, he becomes king, and even wins the support of his brothers by his kindness and generosity.

Also note the significance of the white umbrella. In ancient India justice was dispensed under a tree. Later the umbrella replaced the tree (because of the hot sun) both physically and symbolically. Therefore the umbrella was the symbol for justice. Buddhism adopted this symbolism and in the 200 years or so after the Buddha died he is sometimes represented by an umbrella, a throne, and two footprints with a Dharma wheel inside of them.

The themes of this Jātaka are patience and gratitude.

"Their heart's desire." This story was told by the Master while at Jetavana about a monk who gave up persevering. In this Jātaka both the Introductory Story and the Story of the Past will be given in the Eleventh Book in connection with the Saṃvara Jātaka. The incidents are the same both for that Jātaka and for this, but the stanzas are different.

By following the advice of the Bodhisatta, Prince Gāmani, even though he was the youngest of a hundred brothers, found himself surrounded by those hundred brothers as a retinue and seated beneath the white canopy of kingship. He contemplated his glory and thought, "All this glory I owe to my teacher." And, in his joy, he burst into this heartfelt utterance:

8: Gāmani Jātaka, Prince Gāmani

Their heart's desire they reap, who hurry not.
Know, Gāmani, ripe excellence is thine.

Seven or eight days after he became the King, all his brothers departed to their own homes. King Gāmani, after ruling his kingdom in righteousness, passed away to fare according to his karma. The Bodhisatta also passed away to fare according to his karma.

Figure: King Gāmani

His lesson ended, the Master preached the Dharma, after which the faint-hearted monk won Arahatship. Having told the two stories, the

Master showed the connection linking them both together and identified the birth.

9: Makhādeva Jātaka,
King Makhādeva

This is the ultimate mid-life crisis story. While this story is a little extreme (!), the contemplation of death is a regular theme in the Buddha's teaching. It is used as a reminder that our time in this life is short, and we should not waste it.

We usually think of renunciation as giving up the pleasures of worldly life. But those pleasures also come with a price. So a different way of thinking about renunciation is that you are giving up the stress and suffering that comes with seeking worldly, sensual pleasures and cultivating a higher and more deeply satisfying kind of pleasure. As the King says, "I have had my fill of human joys and would rather taste divine joys."

"Oh, these gray hairs!" This story was told by the Master while at Jetavana about the Great Renunciation, which has already been related in the Nidāna Kathā. (*"The Story of Origins." The Nidāna Kathā is an introductory text to the Jātakas but also stands on its own. It tells the story of all the Buddha's previous lives starting from when he was inspired to become a Buddha.*)

On this occasion the monks sat praising the renunciation of the Lord of Wisdom. Entering the Dharma Hall and seating himself on the Buddha-seat, the Master thus addressed the monks. "What were you just discussing?"

"We were praising, sir, your own renunciation."

"Monks," responded the Master, "not only in these days have I made a renunciation, in past days I similarly renounced the world."

The monks asked the Blessed One for an explanation of this. The Blessed One made clear what had been concealed from them by rebirth.

Once on a time in Mithilā in the realm of Videha there was a King named Makhādeva, who was righteous and ruled righteously. For successive periods of eighty-four thousand years he had respectively amused himself as prince, ruled as viceroy, and then reigned as King. One day he said to his barber, "Tell me, friend barber, when you see any gray hairs in my head."

So one day, years and years later, the barber did find among the raven locks of the King a single gray hair, and he told the King so. "Pull it out, my friend," said the King, "and put it in the palm of my hand." The barber plucked the hair out with his golden tongs and laid it in the King's hand. The King at that time still had eighty-four thousand years more to live. But nevertheless, at the sight of that one gray hair he was filled with deep emotion. He seemed to see the King of Death standing over him. "Foolish Makhādeva!" he cried. "Gray hairs have come upon you before you have been able to rid yourself of defilements." And as he thought about the appearance of his gray hair, he grew hot within. The sweat rolled down from his body, and suddenly his clothing oppressed him and seemed intolerable.

Figure: The Gray Hair!

9: Makhādeva Jātaka, King Makhādeva

"Today," he thought, "I will renounce the world for the life of a monk."

He gave the grant of a village to his barber, which yielded a hundred thousand pieces of money. He sent for his eldest son and said to him, "My son, gray hairs have come upon me, and I am old. I have had my fill of human joys and would rather taste divine joys. The time for my renunciation has come. Take the sovereignty upon yourself. As for me, I will take up my abode in the pleasure garden called Makhādeva's Mango-grove, and there I will tread the path of a spiritual seeker."

At this his ministers gathered and said, "Why, sire, are you taking up the life of a monk?"

Taking the gray hair in his hand, the King repeated this stanza:

> Lo, these gray hairs that on my head appear
> Are Death's own messengers that come to rob
> My life. 'Tis time I turned from worldly things,
> And in the hermit's path seek saving peace.

And after these words, he renounced his sovereignty and became a recluse. Dwelling in that very Mango-grove of Makhādeva, over the next eighty-four thousand years he cultivated the Four Perfect States (*love, compassion, empathetic joy, and equanimity*) within himself, and, dying with insight full and unbroken, was reborn in the Brahma Realm. After passing from there, he became the King again in Mithilā under the name of Nimi. After uniting his scattered family, once more became a hermit in that same Mango-grove, winning the Four Perfect States and passing on once more to the Realm of Brahma.

After repeating his statement that he had similarly renounced the world in bygone days, the Master at the end of his lesson preached the Four Noble Truths. Some entered the First Path (*stream-entry*), some the Second (*once-returner*), and some the Third (*non-returner*). Having told the two stories, the Master showed the connection between them and identified the birth, by saying: "In those days Ānanda was the barber, Rāhula the son, and I myself King Makhādeva." (*Ānanda was the Buddha's cousin and his attendant, and Rāhula really was his son.*)

10: Sukhavihāri Jātaka,
Dwelling in Happiness

The story of Bhaddiya is one of the iconic stories of Buddhism. It points to the delight, freedom, and happiness that can come from Buddhist practice and the monastic way of life. The aim of the Buddha's teachings is to find precisely the kind of joy that Bhaddiya finds.

The first time that I heard this story I was at a retreat with Thich Nhat Hanh. Thây, as his students call him, has a beautiful, poetic way of being, and he speaks in a wonderfully clipped Viet Namese accent. Whenever I think of this story I still hear it in his voice.

This story is told – slightly differently - in other places in the Pāli Canon as well. (Udāna 2.10, Cullavaga 7.1.5, Therigatha 16.7)

"*The un-guarded man.*" This story was told by the Master while in the Anūpiya Mango-grove near the town of Anūpiya. It is about the Elder Bhaddiya (the Happy), who joined the Saṅgha in the company of the six young nobles and their barber Upāli. Of these the Elders Bhaddiya, Kimbila, Bhagu, and Upāli attained to Arahatship. The Elder Ānanda entered the First Path (*stream-entry*), the Elder Anuruddha gained all-seeing vision, and Devadatta obtained the power of ecstatic self-abstraction. The story of the six young nobles, up to the events at Anūpiya, will be related in the Khaṇḍahāla Jātaka (*Jātaka 542*).

(*The six nobles were cousins of the Buddha. Upāli became foremost in mastery of the Vinaya, the rules of conduct for the monks. Devadatta eventually turned on the Buddha. He tried to take over the Saṅgha and even tried to murder the Buddha.*)

The venerable Bhaddiya used to be a member of the royal family. He was always in danger and had to guard himself as though he were his own protector deity. He had many soldiers, but even so he had trouble sleeping even on his royal couch in his private apartments high up in the palace. Now that he was an Arahat, he roamed in forests and desert places without any fear at all. And at that thought he burst into this heartfelt utterance, "Oh, happiness! Oh, happiness!"

The monks reported this to the Blessed One, saying, "The venerable Bhaddiya is declaring the bliss he has won." (*According to the monastic*

10: Sukhavihāri Jātaka, Dwelling in Happiness

code monks and nuns are not supposed to declare any attainments they have.)

"Monks," said the Blessed One, "this is not the first time that Bhaddiya's life has been happy. His life was no less happy in bygone days."

The monks asked the Blessed One to explain this. The Blessed One made clear what had been concealed from them by rebirth.

Once upon a time when Brahmadatta was reigning in Benares, the Bodhisatta was born as a wealthy northern brahmin. Realizing the dangers in sense pleasures and the blessings that flow from renouncing the world, he abandoned sense pleasures and retired to the Himalayas. He became a recluse there and won the eight attainments (*the eight jhānas, or states of mental absorption*). He gained many followers, amounting to 500 monks. Once when the rainy season started, he left the Himalayas and went on an alms pilgrimage with his followers through village and town and at last came to Benares. There he stayed in the royal pleasure garden as the beneficiary of the King's generosity. After living here for the four months of the rainy season, he went to the King to bid him good-bye. But the King said to him, "You are old, reverend sir. Why go back to the Himalayas? Send your pupils back and stay here."

The Bodhisatta entrusted his 500 ascetics to the care of his oldest disciple, saying, "Go back to the Himalayas. I will stay here."

Now that oldest disciple had once been a king, but he had given up a mighty kingdom to become a monk. By practicing meditative concentration, he was able to master the eight jhānas. As he lived with the ascetics in the Himalayas, one day he longed to see the Master. He said to his companions, "Live on contentedly here. I will come back as soon as I have paid my respects to the Master." So he went to the Master, paid his respects to him, and greeted him lovingly. Then he lay down by the side of his Master on a mat that he spread there.

At this point the King appeared. He had come to the pleasure garden to see the disciple. With a salutation, he took his seat on one side. But though he was aware of the King's presence, that oldest disciple did not rise, but still lay there, crying with passionate earnestness, "Oh, happiness! Oh, happiness!"

Displeased that the disciple had not risen, the King said to the Bodhisatta, "Reverend sir, this monk must have had his fill to eat, seeing that he continues to lie there so happily exclaiming with such earnestness." (*Apparently the King had brought alms food.*)

"Sire," said the Bodhisatta, "this monk used to be a king as you are. He is thinking how in the old days when he was a layman, he lived in regal pomp with many soldiers to guard him. But he never knew the happiness that he now has. It is the happiness of the monk's life and the happiness that insight brings that move him to this heartfelt utterance." And the Bodhisatta repeated this poem to further teach the King the Dharma:

The man who guards not, nor is guarded, sire,
Lives happy, freed from slavery to lust.

Figure: Oh, happiness!

Appeased by the lesson, the King made his salutation and returned to his palace. The disciple also left his Master and returned to the Himalayas. The Bodhisatta continued to live there until he died, with insight full and unbroken. He was then reborn in the Brahma realm.

His lesson ended, and the two stories told, the Master showed the connection linking them both together. He identified the birth by saying, "The Elder Bhaddiya was the disciple of those days, and I myself the Master of the company of monks."

* * *

2:10 Bhaddiya Kāḷigodha,
(Kāḷigodha Sutta)

Translated by Ṭhānissaro Bhikkhu

This is such a wonderful story that I have chosen to include another version of it from the Pāli Canon. This is from the Udāna. In the Pāli Canon there are five collections. The fifth collection is the Khuddaka Nikāya. The Khuddaka Nikāya has either 18 volumes (Burmese version) or 15 volumes (non-Burmese version) depending on the version. The Udāna ("Exclamations") and the Jātaka Tales are both in the Khuddaka Nikāya. The Udāna is available for free as an eBook at Dhammatalks.org.

I have heard that on one occasion the Blessed One was staying near Anupiyā in the Mango Grove. And on that occasion, Ven. Bhaddiya, Kāḷigodhā's son, on going to the wilderness, to the root of a tree, or to an empty dwelling, would repeatedly exclaim, "What bliss! What bliss!"

A large number of monks heard Ven. Bhaddiya, Kāḷigodhā's son, on going to the wilderness, to the root of a tree, or to an empty dwelling, repeatedly exclaim, "What bliss! What bliss!" and on hearing him, the thought occurred to them, "There's no doubt but that Ven. Bhaddiya, Kāḷigodhā's son, doesn't enjoy leading the holy life, for when he was a householder he knew the bliss of kingship, so that now, on recollecting that when going to the wilderness, to the root of a tree, or to an empty dwelling, he is repeatedly exclaiming, 'What bliss! What bliss!'"

So they went to the Blessed One and, on arrival, having bowed down to him, sat to one side. As they were sitting there, they told him, "Ven. Bhaddiya, Kāḷigodhā's son, lord, on going to the wilderness, to the root of a tree, or to an empty dwelling, repeatedly exclaims, 'What bliss.'"

Then the Blessed One told a certain monk, "Come, monk. In my name, call Bhaddiya, saying, 'The Teacher calls you, friend Bhaddiya.'"

Responding, "As you say, lord," to the Blessed One, the monk went to Ven. Bhaddiya, Kāḷigodhā's son, and on arrival he said to him, "The Teacher calls you, friend Bhaddiya."

Responding, "As you say, my friend," to the monk, Ven. Bhaddiya, Kāḷigodhā's son, went to the Blessed One and, on arrival, having bowed down to him, sat to one side. As he was sitting there, the Blessed One said to him, "Is it true, Bhaddiya that on going to the wilderness, to the root of a tree, or to an empty dwelling, you repeatedly exclaim, 'What bliss! What bliss!'?"

"Yes, lord."

"What compelling reason do you have in mind that when going to the wilderness, to the root of a tree, or to an empty dwelling, you repeatedly exclaim, 'What bliss! What bliss!'?"

"Before, when I has a householder, maintaining the bliss of kingship, lord, I had guards posted within and without the royal apartments, within and without the city, within and without the countryside. But even though I was thus guarded, thus protected, I lived in fear – agitated, distrustful, and afraid. But now, on going alone to the wilderness, to the root of a tree, or to an empty dwelling, I live without fear, un-agitated, confident, and unafraid – unconcerned, unruffled, living on the gifts of others, with my mind like a wild deer. This is the compelling reason I have in mind that – when going to the wilderness, to the root of a tree, or to an empty dwelling – I repeatedly exclaim, 'What bliss! What bliss!'"

Then, on realizing the significance of that, the Blessed One on that occasion exclaimed:

> *From whose heart*
> *there is no provocation,*
> *and for whom becoming and non-becoming*
> > *are overcome,*
> *he –*
> > *beyond fear,*
> > *blissful,*
> > *with no grief –*
> *is one the devas can't see.*

11: Lakkhaṇa Jātaka,
The Honorable Man

This is another Jātaka Tale where Devadatta gets pretty rough treatment. You may recall that Devadatta was the Buddha's cousin and a monk. He challenged the Buddha in order to take over the Saṅgha and even tried to kill him. It seems probable that the purpose of these stories is to make Devadatta appear as evil as possible.

"The honorable man." This story about Devadatta was told by the Master in the Bamboo-grove near Rājagaha. The story of Devadatta will be related, up to the date of the Abhimāra employment in the Khaṇḍahāla Jātaka, up to the date of his dismissal from the office of Treasurer in the Cullahaṃsa Jātaka, and, up to the date of his being swallowed up by the earth in the Sixteenth Book in the Samudda-vāṇija Jātaka.

(*The incidents listed here are various stories in Devadatta's life.*)

On the occasion now in question, Devadatta, failing to get the Buddha to agree to the Five Points (*Devadatta challenged the Buddha's authority by trying to get him to agree that all monks 1) should live all their lives in the forest, 2) live entirely on alms obtained by begging, 3) wear only robes made of discarded rags, 4) live at the foot of a tree and 5) abstain completely from eating meat*), caused a schism in the Saṅgha. He went off with five hundred monks to live at Gayāsīsa. The Master called his two chief disciples (*Sāriputta and Moggallāna*) and said, "Sāriputta, the five hundred pupils who were perverted by Devadatta's teaching went off with him. Go with some members of the Saṅgha, preach the Dharma to them, enlighten these wanderers respecting the Paths and the Fruits, and bring them back with you."

They did as they were asked, preached the Dharma, enlightened the wayward monks respecting the Paths and the Fruits, and came back the next day at dawn with the five hundred monks to the Bamboo-grove. And while Sāriputta was standing there after saluting the Blessed One on his return, the monks spoke to him in praise of the Elder Sāriputta. "Sir, the glory of our elder brother was very bright as he returned with a following of five hundred monks, whereas Devadatta has lost all his followers."

"This is not the only time, monks, when Sāriputta gained glory after returning with those for whom he is responsible. This happened in the past as well. Likewise, this is not the only time when Devadatta lost his following."

The monks asked the Blessed One to explain this to them. The Blessed One made clear what had been concealed by rebirth.

Once upon a time in the city of Rājagaha in the kingdom of Magadha there ruled a certain king of Magadha. In those days the Bodhisatta came to life as a buck. Growing up, he lived in the forest as the leader of a herd of a thousand deer. He had two young bucks named Luckie and Blackie. When he grew old, he divided his herd in two. He handed his herd over to his two sons, placing five hundred deer under the care of each of them. And so now these two young bucks were in charge of the herd.

At harvest time in Magadha, when the crops stand thick in the fields, it is dangerous for the deer in the surrounding forests. The peasants are anxious to kill the animals that eat their crops. They dig pitfalls, fix stakes, set stone-traps, and plant snares and other traps, so that many deer are killed.

Accordingly, when the Bodhisatta saw that it was crop time, he sent for his two sons and said to them, "My children, it is now the time when crops stand thick in the fields, and many deer meet their death at this season. We who are old will stay here, but you will each take your herd to the mountainous tracts in the forest and come back when the crops have been harvested."

"Very good," said his two sons, and they departed with their herds as their father had asked.

Now the men who live along the route know quite well the times at which deer take to the hills and then return. They lie in wait in hiding places here and there, and they shoot and kill many of them. The dullard Blackie, ignorant of the times to travel and the times to stop, kept his deer on the march early and late, both at dawn and at dusk, approaching the very edges of the villages. And the peasants, in ambush or in the open, destroyed many of his herd. Having caused the destruction of so many deer, he reached the forest with very few survivors.

11: Lakkhaṇa Jātaka,
The Honorable Man

Luckie on the other hand, being wise and astute and resourceful, never approached the edges of a village. He did not travel by day, or even in the dawn or at dusk. He only moved in the dead of night. As a result, he reached the forest without losing a single head of his deer.

Figure: Luckie Protecting the Herd

They stayed in the forest for four months, not leaving the hills until the crops were harvested. On the way back Blackie repeated his folly and lost the rest of his herd. He returned home solitary and alone. But Luckie had not lost one of his deer. He brought back all five hundred of them. As he saw his two sons returning, the Bodhisatta composed this stanza about the herd of deer:

The upright kindly man gets his reward.
See Luckie leading back his troop of kin,
While here comes Blackie bereft of all his herd.

And this was how the Bodhisatta welcomed his sons. And after living to a ripe old age, he passed away to fare according to his karma.

At the end of his lesson, when the Master had repeated that Sāriputta's glory and Devadatta's loss both had had a parallel in bygone days, he showed the connection linking the two stories together. He identified the birth by saying, "Devadatta was the Blackie of those days. His followers were Blackie's following. Sāriputta was Luckie of those days, and his following were the Buddha's followers. Rāhula's mother was the mother of those days, and I myself was the father."

12: Nigrodhamiga Jātaka,
Keep Only with the Banyan Deer

This Jātaka is the first one in the collection about a nun. Women at the time of the Buddha were little more than slaves. But the Buddha not only started an order of nuns, there were many prominent laywomen in his Saṅgha. One of them, Visākhā, is also in this story.

Also notice that the Buddha does not automatically take the nun into his Saṅgha. Even though he knows that she is innocent of any wrong-doing, he is sensitive to the realities of public opinion. The monks and nuns lived on alms food. They were completely at the mercy of the support of the community. So he organized a process whereby her innocence could be shown in a public way.

I am sure you will not miss the unflattering description of the human body. One of the strongest attachments we have and one of the strongest senses of self-identity that we have is with the human body. This creates a lot of suffering for ourselves and is an important focus in Buddhist practice. The aim is to appreciate and care for the body without becoming attached to it as "me."

"Keep only with the Banyan Deer." This story was told by the Master while at Jetavana. It is about the mother of the Elder Prince Kassapa. She was the daughter, we learn, of a wealthy merchant of Rājagaha. She was deeply rooted in goodness, and she scorned all worldly things. She had reached her final existence and within her breast, like a lamp in a pitcher, the certainty of her winning Arahatship glowed.

Even at a very young age, she took no joy in a worldly life. She yearned to renounce the world and to become a nun. With this aim, she said to her mother and father, "My dear parents, my heart takes no joy in a worldly life. I would rather embrace the saving Dharma of the Buddha. Let me take the vows."

"What, my dear? We are a very wealthy family, and you are our only daughter. You cannot take the vows."

Even though she asked them again and again, she failed to win her parents' consent. She thought to herself, "So be it. When I am married into another family, I will get my husband's consent and take the vows."

When she came of age, she entered another family. She proved a devoted wife and lived a life of goodness and virtue in her new home. Now it came to pass that she became pregnant, but she did not know it.

There was a festival proclaimed in that city, and everybody kept the holiday. The city was decorated like a city of the gods. But even at the height of the festival, she did not wear any jewelry or fine clothes. Her husband said to her, "My dear wife, everybody is on holiday, but you do not put on your best clothes."

"My lord and master," she replied, "the body is filled with thirty-two parts. Why should it be decorated? This body is not sacred. It is not made of gold, jewels, or yellow sandal-wood. It does not take its birth from the womb of lotus-flowers, white or red or blue. It is not filled with any immortal balsam. No. It is bred of corruption and born of mortal parents. The qualities that mark it are the wearing and wasting away, the decay and destruction of the merely transient. It is destined to swell a graveyard and is devoted to lust. It is the source of sorrow and lamentation. It is the home of all diseases, and the storehouse of the workings of karma. It is foul inside and always excreting. Yes, as all the world can see, its end is death, passing to the cemetery, there to be the habitat of worms. What would I gain, my bridegroom, by ornamenting this body? Wouldn't that be like decorating a latrine?"

"My dear wife," responded the young merchant, "if you think this body is so foul, why don't you become a nun?"

"If I am accepted, my husband, I will take the vows this very day."

"Very good," he said. "I will get you admitted to the Saṅgha." And after he gave wonderful gifts and showed hospitality to the Saṅgha, he escorted her with a large following to the monastery and had her admitted as a nun, but of the Saṅgha of Devadatta. Nonetheless, she felt great joy at the fulfillment of her desire to become a nun.

As time went on the other nuns noticed her getting larger. She had swelling in her hands and feet. They said, "Lady, it looks like you are about to become a mother. What does it mean?"

"I cannot tell you, sisters. I only know I have led a virtuous life."

So the sisters brought her before Devadatta, saying, "Lord, this young gentle-woman, who was admitted as a sister with the reluctant

12: Nigrodhamiga Jātaka,
Keep Only with the Banyan Deer

consent of her husband, has now proven to be with child. But whether this happened before her admission to the Saṅgha or not, we cannot say. What should we do now?"

Not being a Buddha and not having any charity, love, or compassion, Devadatta thought, "It will damage my reputation if one of my nuns is pregnant and I forgive the offense. My course is clear. I must expel her from the Saṅgha." Without any investigation into what had happened, he started forward as if to thrust aside a mass of stone and said, "Away, and expel this woman!"

The sisters arose and with reverent salutation withdrew to their own nunnery. But the girl said to those sisters, "Ladies, Devadatta the Elder is not the Buddha. My real vows were not taken under Devadatta, but under the Buddha, the Foremost of the world. Do not rob me of the path I won with such difficulty. Take me before the Master at Jetavana." So they set out with her for Jetavana, and traveling over one hundred fifty miles from Rājagaha, they arrived at their destination. There they saluted the Master and told him what had happened.

The Master thought, "Although the child was conceived while she was still a layperson, it will give Devadatta's followers an excuse to say that the ascetic Gotama has taken a sister expelled by Devadatta. Therefore, to cut short such talk, this case must be heard in the presence of the King and his court."

So the next day he sent for Pasenadi, King of Kosala, the elder and the younger Anāthapiṇḍika, the lady Visākhā, the great lay-disciple, and other well-known people. In the evening, when the four classes of the faithful were all assembled - monks, nuns, laymen, and laywomen - he said to the Elder Upāli, "Go, and clear up the matter of the young sister in the presence of the four classes of my disciples."

"It shall be done, reverend sir," said the Elder, and he went before the assembly. Seating himself in his place, he called up Visākhā, the lay-disciple, in sight of the King. He placed the conduct of the inquiry in her hands, saying, "First determine the precise day and month on which this girl joined the Saṅgha, Visākhā. Then determine whether she conceived before or after that date."

Accordingly the lady had a curtain put up as a screen, behind which she went with the girl. Visākhā determined that the conception had taken place before the girl had become a nun. She reported this to the

Elder, who proclaimed the sister innocent before the assembly. And now that her innocence was established, she reverently saluted the Sangha and the Master, and she returned with the sisters to her own nunnery.

When her time came, she bore a son who was strong in spirit, for she had prayed at the feet of the Buddha Padumuttara (*a previous Buddha*) ages ago. One day, when the King was passing by the nunnery, he heard the cry of an infant and asked his courtiers what it meant. They told his majesty that the cry came from the child to which the young sister had given birth. "Sirs," said the King, "the care of children is a burden to sisters in their holy life. Let us take charge of him." So by the King's command the infant was handed over to the ladies of his family and raised as a prince. When the day came for him to be named, he was named Kassapa. But he was known as Prince Kassapa because he was brought up like a prince.

At the age of seven he became a novice monk under the Master, and he became a full monk when he was old enough. As time went on, he became famous as an expounder of the Dharma. So the Master gave him a special status, saying, "Monks, Prince Kassapa is foremost in the Sangha in eloquence." Afterwards, by virtue of the Vammīka Sutta [MN 23] he won Arahatship. His mother also grew to clear vision and became an Arahat. Prince Kassapa the Elder shone in the faith of the Buddha even as the full moon in the mid-heaven.

Now one afternoon when the Tathāgata was returning from his alms-round, he addressed the Sangha then went into his perfumed chamber. After his address the monks spent the daytime either in their night-quarters or in their day-quarters until it was evening. When they assembled in the Dharma hall, they said, "Brothers, Devadatta is not a Buddha, and because he had no charity, love, or compassion, he could have ruined the lives of the Elder Prince Kassapa and his reverend mother. But the All-enlightened Buddha, being the Lord of the Dharma and being perfect in charity, love, and compassion, has been their salvation."

And as they sat there singing the praises of the Buddha, he entered the hall with all the grace of a Buddha, and asked, as he took his. seat, what they were talking about.

12: Nigrodhamiga Jātaka,
Keep Only with the Banyan Deer

"Of your own virtues, sir," they said, and told him what they had been discussing.

"This is not the first time, brothers," he said, "that the Tathāgata has proved the salvation and refuge of these two. He did in the past as well."

The brothers asked him to explain this to them, and he told them what rebirth had hidden from them.

Once upon a time, when Brahmadatta was reigning in Benares, the Bodhisatta was born as a deer. His fir was the color of gold. His eyes were like round jewels. His horns were silver. His mouth was red as a bunch of scarlet cloth. His four hoofs looked like they were lacquered. His tail was soft and fluffy like a yak's, and he was as big as a young foal. Attended by five hundred deer, he lived in the forest under the name of King Banyan Deer. And nearby him lived another deer who also had a herd of five hundred deer. His name was Branch Deer, and his fir was as gold as the Bodhisatta.

In those days the King of Benares was very fond of hunting, and he always had meat at every meal. Every day he gathered all of his subjects, townsfolk and country folk alike, to the detriment of their business, and went hunting. His people thought, "This King stops all of our work. Suppose we were to plant food and supply water for the deer in his own pleasure garden. Then we could drive in a number of deer, corral them and deliver them over to the King!"

So they planted grass in the pleasure garden for the deer to eat and supplied water for them to drink and opened up the gate. Then they called out the townsfolk and went into the forest armed with sticks and all manner of weapons to find the deer. They surrounded a large portion of forest to catch the deer within their circle, and in so doing surrounded the places where Banyan and Branch deer were. As soon as they saw the deer, they beat the trees, bushes and ground with their sticks until they drove the herds out of their sanctuaries. Then they rattled their swords and spears and bows with such noise that they drove all the deer into the pleasure garden, and they shut the gate. Then they went to the King and said, "Sire, you put a stop to our work by always going hunting. So we have driven enough deer from the forest to fill your pleasure garden. From now on feed on them."

After this the King went to the pleasure garden. Looking over the herd, he saw the two golden deer. He granted them immunity.

After that, sometimes the King would go on his own and shoot a deer to bring home. Sometimes his cook would go and shoot one. At first sight of the bow, the deer would dash off trembling for their lives, but after receiving two or three wounds they grew weak and faint and died. The herd of deer told this to the Bodhisatta, who sent for Branch and said, "Friend, the deer are being destroyed in large numbers. At least let them not be needlessly wounded and suffer so much. Let the deer go to the chopping block by turns, one day one from my herd, and next day one from yours. The deer will then go to the place of execution and lie down with its head on the block. In this way the deer will escape being wounded." Branch agreed, and after that the deer whose turn it was would go and lie down with its neck ready on the block. The cook used to go and carry off only the victim that was there for him.

Now one day it was the turn of a pregnant doe of Branch's herd, and she went to Branch and said, "Lord, I am with child. When my little one is born, we will both take our turn. But please allow me to be passed over this turn."

"No, I cannot have another take your turn," he said. "You must bear the consequences of your own fortune. Be gone!"

Having failed with him, the doe went to the Bodhisatta and told him her story. He answered, "Very well. You go away, and I will see that you skip your turn."

And then he went himself to the place of execution and lay down with his head on the chopping block. On seeing him the cook cried, "Why here's the king of the deer who was granted immunity! What does this mean?" And he ran off to tell the King. The moment he heard of it, the King mounted his chariot and arrived with a large following. "My friend the king of the deer," he said, "Didn't I promise to spare your life? Why are you lying here?"

"Sire, a doe came to me. She is with child, and she begged me to let her skip her turn. And since I could not pass the doom of one on to another, I will lay down my life for her and take her doom on myself. Do not think that there is anything behind this, your majesty."

12: Nigrodhamiga Jātaka,
Keep Only with the Banyan Deer

Figure: The King and Banyan Deer

"My lord the golden king of the deer," said the King, "I have never seen anyone, even among men, so full of charity, love, and compassion as you. Therefore, I am pleased with you. Arise! I spare the lives of both you and her."

"What about the rest of the deer, O King of men?"

"I spare their lives too, my lord."

"Sire, only the deer in your pleasure garden will have immunity. What about all the other deer?"

"I spare their lives, too, my lord."

"Sire, the deer will then be safe, but what about the rest of four-footed creatures?"

"I spare their lives too, my lord."

"Sire, four-footed creatures will then be safe, but what about the flocks of birds"

"They will also be spared, my lord."

"Sire, birds will then be safe, but what about the fish, those who live in the water?"

"I also spare their lives, my lord."

Having interceded on behalf of all living creatures, the Bodhisatta arose, established the King in the Five Precepts and said, "Walk in righteousness, great King. Walk in righteousness and justice towards parents, children, townsmen, and country folk, so that when this earthly body is dissolved, you may enter the bliss of heaven."

Thus, with the grace and charm that marks a Buddha, he taught the Dharma to the King. He stayed for a few days in the pleasure garden in order to instruct him, and then with his attendant herd he went into the forest again.

That doe gave birth to a fawn as fair as the opening bud of the lotus. He used to play about with the Branch deer. Seeing this his mother said to him, "My child, don't go about with him, only go about with the herd of the Banyan deer." And in order to persuade him, she repeated this stanza:

> Keep only with the Banyan deer, and shun
> The Branch deer's herd; more welcome far
> Is death, my child, in Banyan's company,
> Than even the most bountiful life with Branch.

Afterwards the deer, now enjoying immunity, used to eat men's crops, and the men, remembering the immunity granted to them, did not dare to hit the deer or drive them away. So they assembled in the King's courtyard and put the matter before him. He said, "When the Banyan deer won my favor, I promised him a boon. I would rather give up my kingdom than break my promise. Be gone! No one in my kingdom may harm the deer."

But when Banyan heard about this, he called his herd together and said, "From now on you will not eat the crops of men." And having done this, he sent a message to the men, saying, "From this day on, do not fence your fields, but merely mark the boundaries with leaves tied up around them." And so, we hear, the custom began of tying up leaves to indicate the boundaries of the fields. And after that a deer

12: Nigrodhamiga Jātaka,
Keep Only with the Banyan Deer

was never known to trespass on a field marked in that way for they had been instructed by the Bodhisatta.

This is how the Bodhisatta ruled the deer of his herd, and this is how he acted all his life. At the end of a long life he passed away to fare according to his karma. The King too lived by the Bodhisatta's teachings, and after a life spent in good works passed away to fare according to his karma.

At the close of this lesson, the Master repeated that, as now, in bygone days he had also been the salvation of the mother and her son. Then he preached the Four Noble Truths and showed the connection, linking the two stories he had told together. He identified the birth by saying, "Devadatta was the Branch deer of those days, and his followers were that deer's herd. The nun was the doe, and Prince Kassapa was her son. Ānanda was the King, and I was King Banyan Deer."

13: Kaṇḍina Jātaka,
The Mountain Buck

The original translation of this Jātaka is quite misogynistic. Although the Buddha took the radical step of ordaining women, and he went to great lengths to protect them, his equal treatment of women was very unpopular. Over the years this resentment crept into the Pāli Canon. You find much less of this in the Chinese versions of the canon, the Agamas. This is what makes the authenticity of the sexism suspect.

This Jātaka takes on one of the Buddha's most radical – and equally unpopular – topics, and that is how sense desire causes suffering. Most people think that it is self-evident that happiness in life is about pleasing the senses through food, sex, etc. The Buddha taught that a) chasing sense pleasure is a major source of our suffering and b) that there is a greater happiness that can come from within. This happiness does not cause the harm or have the risks that chasing sense pleasures has, and it can be cultivated by developing the mind.

"*Cursed is the arrow of passion.*" This story was told by the Master while at Jetavana about the temptation caused to monks by the wives of their worldly life. There was one monk in particular who was obsessed with his worldly wife. The Blessed One said to him, "Brother, it was because of this very woman that in bygone days you met your death and were roasted over glowing embers." The brothers asked the Blessed One to explain this. The Blessed One made clear what had been concealed from them by rebirth.

Once upon a time in the kingdom of Magadha the King was reigning in Rājagaha, and when the crops were grown the deer were exposed to great perils so they retired to the forest. Now a certain mountain buck of the forest, having become enamored of a doe who came from near a village, was moved by his infatuation with her to accompany her when the deer returned home from the forest. She said, "You, sir, are but a simple buck of the forest. Where I live near the village is full of with peril and danger. So don't come down with us." But because of his great passion for her, he would not stay, but went with her.

When the villagers knew that it was the time for the deer to come down from the hills, the people of Magadha set an ambush by the

13: Kaṇḍina Jātaka,
The Mountain Buck

road. A hunter was lying in wait just by the road along which the pair were traveling. The young doe smelled the man's scent and suspected that a hunter was in ambush. So she let the buck go first and followed behind at some distance. With a single arrow the hunter killed the buck, and seeing this, the doe ran off like the wind. Then that hunter came out of his hiding place and skinned the buck, lit a fire, and cooked the sweet flesh over the embers. Having eaten and drunk, he took home the remainder of the bleeding carcass on his carrying-pole to provide a feast for his children.

Figure: The Infatuated Buck

Now in those days the Bodhisatta was a fairy living in that very grove of trees, and he saw what had happened. "It was passion that destroyed this foolish deer. At the start passion is bliss, but its end is sorrow and suffering. To cause another's death is an act of evil in this world. Infamy also rules in a land where a man succumbs to desire for a woman and men yield to passion for a woman."

And then, while the other fairies of the wood applauded and offered perfumes and flowers and the like in homage, the Bodhisatta wove the three infamies into a single stanza, and made the wood re-echo with his sweet tones as he taught the truth in these lines:

Cursed be the arrow of passion that creates such pain!
Cursed be the land where passion rules supreme!
And cursed the fool that bows to passion's sway!

Thus the Buddha composed in a single stanza these three infamies, and the woods re-echoed as he taught the Dharma with all the mastery and grace of a Buddha.

His lesson ended, the Master preached the Four Noble Truths. At the close of this the love-sick monk was established in the Fruit of the First Path (*stream-entry*). Having told the two stories, the Master showed the connection linking the two together, and identified the birth.

"In those days," said the Master, "the love-sick brother was the mountain buck. His wife was the young doe, and I was the fairy who preached the Dharma showing the dangers of passion."

14: Vātamiga Jātaka,
The Greedy Antelope

This is another Jātaka where the theme is the danger inherent in sense pleasures, or perhaps more subtly the lust for sense pleasures. Sometimes it is more the craving, not the actual sense pleasure, that is the problem. We are slaves to our sense desires, and this leads to a great deal of unskillful behavior and a lot of suffering.

"There's nothing worse." This story was told by the Master while at Jetavana. It is about the Elder Tissa, also called The Forest Dweller. Tradition says that while the Master was living at the Bamboo-grove near Rājagaha, the descendent of a wealthy family, Prince Tissa by name, came to visit. The Master inspired him by giving a discourse, and so he decided to join the Saṅgha. But his parents refused to give their consent. He finally obtained it by following Raṭṭhapāla's example and refusing food for seven days, after which they allowed him to take vows with the Master. (*In MN 82 Raṭṭhapāla gained his reluctant parent's approval to become a monk by refusing to eat or drink until either he died or they gave their permission.*)

Two weeks after admitting this young man, the Master left the Bamboo-grove and went to Jetavana. There the young nobleman undertook the Thirteen Obligations (*these are special, optional Precepts*). He passed his time by going on alms rounds from house to house, omitting none. Under the name of Elder Tissa The Forest Dweller, he became as bright and shining a light in Buddhism as the moon in the vault of heaven.

At this time there was a festival at Rājagaha. The Elder Tissa's mother and father put the trinkets he used to wear as a layman into a silver casket. They bemoaned, "At other festivals our son used to wear these fine clothes, but the sage Gotama took him, our only son, to the town of Sāvatthi. Where is our son sitting now or standing?"

Now a slave-girl who came to the house noticed the lady of the house weeping, and she asked her why she was crying. The lady told her everything.

"Madam, what did your son enjoy?"

The lady told her.

"Well, if you will give me authority in this house, I'll get your son back."

"Very good," said the lady. She gave the girl some money and sent her with a large contingent, saying, "Go, and get my son back."

The girl rode away in a palanquin (*a litter for one person carried on shoulders with poles*) to Sāvatthi, where she took up her residence in the street that the Elder often used for alms. Surrounding herself with servants of her own, and never allowing the Elder to see his father's people, she watched until the Elder entered the street. She at once bestowed on him alms of fine food and drink. And once she had enticed him, she got him to come into the house. Then she knew that her gifts of food had put him in her power.

The next time that he came for alms, she pretended to be sick. Her people took the Elder's bowl and invited him to sit down.

When he seated himself, he said, "Where is the lay-sister?"

"She's ill, sir," they said. "But it would make her very happy to see you."

Because he had been seduced by his craving for food, he broke his vow and obligation and went to where the woman was lying. (*The monastic code prohibits a monk from being in the presence of a woman unescorted.*) She told him the reason she had come to Sāvatthi. He was so tempted by the wonderful food and other worldly things that she was able to convince him to leave the Saṅgha. She put him in the palanquin and went back with her large contingent to Rājagaha again.

This story quickly spread. The monks sat in the Dharma Hall discussing the matter, saying, "Sirs, we have heard that a slave-girl has carried off the Elder Tissa the Forest Dweller by tempting him with fine food." Entering the Hall the Master sat down on his jeweled seat, and said, "What, brothers, is the subject of discussion in this gathering?" They told him what had happened.

"Brothers," he said, "this is not the first time that he has fallen under her power in bondage to the craving of taste. In bygone days too, he fell under her power in the same way." And so saying, he told this story of the past.

14: Vātamiga Jātaka,
The Greedy Antelope

Once upon a time when Brahmadatta was the King in Benares, he had a gardener named Sañjaya. One day an antelope wandered into the King's pleasure garden, but as soon as it saw Sañjaya it leapt away. But Sañjaya let it go without frightening the timid creature. After several visits the antelope started to roam about in the pleasure garden. Now the gardener was in the habit of gathering flowers and fruits and taking them to the King every day. The King said to him one day, "Have you noticed anything strange, friend gardener, in the pleasure garden?"

"Only, sir, that an antelope has come into the grounds."

"Do you think you could catch it?"

"Oh, yes," said the gardener. "If I had a little honey, I could bring it right into your majesty's palace!"

The King ordered the honey to be given to the man, and he went off with it to the pleasure garden. He put the honey in the grass in spots often visited by the antelope and then hid. When the antelope came and tasted the honied grass, it was so seduced by the lust of taste that it stopped going anywhere other than the pleasure garden. Marking the success of his trap, the gardener began to show himself gradually. The first day or two that the antelope saw him, he once again leapt away. But he quickly grew used to seeing the gardener. He became more confident, and gradually he started to eat grass from the man's hand. Seeing that he had won the creature's trust, he covered the path as thick as a carpet with broken boughs. Then he tied a gourd full of honey on his shoulder, and sticking a bunch of grass in his waist-cloth, he kept dropping tufts of the honied grass in front of the antelope. Finally, he got it right inside the palace. No sooner was the antelope inside than they shut the door!

Seeing so many men, the antelope dashed back and forth around the hall in fear and trembling for his life. The King came down from his chamber above, and seeing the trembling creature said, "This antelope is so timid that for a whole week it will not revisit a spot where it has so much as seen a man. And if it has once been frightened anywhere, it never goes back there again for its whole life. Yet, seduced by the lust of taste, this wild thing from the jungle has actually come into the palace. Truly, my friends, there is nothing more disgraceful in the world than the lust of taste." And he put his teaching into this stanza:

There's no worse trap, men say, than taste,
Alone or with one's friends. Lo! taste it was
That delivered up to Sañjaya
The wild, jungle-haunting antelope.

And with these words he let the antelope go back to its forest again.

Figure: Seduced by the Lust of Taste

When the Master had ended his lesson and had repeated what he had said about the monk having fallen into that woman's power in bygone days as well as in the present time, he showed the connection. He identified the birth, by saying, "In those days this slave-girl was Sañjaya, The Forest Dweller was the antelope, and I myself was the King of Benares."

15: Kharādiyā Jātaka,
Kharādiyā's Story

One of the things I love about the Buddhist literature is its honesty. This is not a romanticized view of life at the time of the Buddha. The Buddha faced all kinds of troublesome people, many of whom seem all too familiar. In this case it is an "unruly monk." Even the Buddha's own monks did not always listen to him.

This is also a lesson about humility, without which one cannot learn. We live in a time when opinions are highly regarded. People often express their point of view without any information what-so-ever. The book of life is long, but if you only ever listen to yourself, it is like reading the same page over and over again.

"For when a deer." This story was told by the Master while at Jetavana about an unruly monk. Tradition says that this monk was unruly and would not heed admonition. Accordingly, the Master asked him, saying, "Is it true, as they say, that you are unruly and will not heed admonition?"

"It is true, Blessed One," was the reply.

"So too in bygone days," said the Master, "you were unruly and would not heed the admonition of the wise and good, with the result that you were caught in a trap and met your death." And so saying, he told this story of the past.

Once upon a time when Brahmadatta was in Benares, the Bodhisatta was born a deer. He lived in the forest as the head of a herd of deer. His sister Kharādiyā brought her son to him and said, "Brother, this is your nephew. Teach him our tricks of survival." And so she placed her son under the Bodhisatta's care.

The Bodhisatta said to his nephew, "Come at such and such a time and I will give you your first lesson." But the nephew never showed up. And, so on that day, as well as the next seven days he skipped his lesson and fail to learn the survival skills of deer.

One day, as he was roaming about, he was caught in a trap. His mother came and said to the Bodhisatta, "Brother, didn't you teach your nephew our ways of surviving?"

"He was an unteachable rascal," said the Bodhisatta. "Your son failed to learn the tricks of deer." And so, having lost all desire to help the mischievous nephew even in his deadly peril, he repeated this stanza:

For when a deer has four hoofs with which to run
And branching antlers armed with countless points,
And by one of seven tricks he could have saved himself,
I teach him then, Kharādiyā, no more.

Figure: The Unteachable Rascal

But the hunter killed the arrogant deer that was caught in the trap and departed with its flesh.

15: Kharādiyā Jātaka,
Kharādiyā's Story

When the Master had ended this lesson about the unruliness of the monk in bygone days as well as in the present, he showed the connection and identified the birth by saying "In those days this unruly monk was the nephew-deer. Uppalavaṇṇā was the sister, and I myself the deer who gave the admonition." (*Uppalavaṇṇā was one of the most prominent nuns in the Buddha's Saṅgha. She gave a discourse that is in the Saṃyutta Nikāya, number 5.5.*)

16: Tipallattha-miga Jātaka, *The Cunning Deer*

This story is about the Buddha's son Rāhula. When Rāhula was born, the Buddha left that day on his spiritual quest. He returned seven years later, and Rāhula immediately ordained as a novice monk. In this story he must still be very young because he is still a novice.

In the last Jātaka we hear the story of a young monk who will not listen to his elders. As a result, he was killed in a previous life. But in this story we see the same situation, but here the young monk is determined to be respectful, listen to his elders, and learn the ways of the wise.

"In all three postures." This story was told by the Master while he was living at the Badarika Monastery in Kosambī. It is about the Elder Rāhula whose heart was intent on observing the rules of the Saṅgha.

Once when the Master was living in the Aggālava Temple near the town of Ālavi, he used to teach in the evenings, after which the senior monks retired to their own huts. But the novice monks and the male lay-disciples lay down to rest in the Dharma hall. When they fell asleep, the snoring was loud and there was snorting and the gnashing of teeth. After a short rest some got up and went to the Blessed One and told him about this improper behavior. He said, "If a monk sleeps in the company of novices, it is a Pācittiya offense (*requiring confession and absolution*)." And after declaring this precept, he went away to Kosambī.

The senior monks said to Rāhula, "Sir, the Blessed One has laid down this precept and now you must find quarters of your own." Before this, the monks, out of respect for the father and because of the anxious desire of the son to observe the rules of the Saṅgha, had welcomed Rāhula as if the place were his. They had fitted up a little bed for him and had given him a cloth to make a pillow with. But on the day of our story they would not give him any space because they were so afraid of breaking the new rule.

However, the excellent Rāhula did not go to the Buddha as his father, nor did he go to Sāriputta (*the Buddha's chief disciple*), Captain of the Faith, who was his preceptor, nor to the Great Moggallāna (*the Buddha's other chief disciple*) who was his teacher, nor to the Elder Ānanda who was his uncle. Instead, he went to the Buddha's outhouse

16: Tipallattha-miga Jātaka,
The Cunning Deer

and took up residence there as though it was a heavenly mansion. Now in a Buddha's outhouse the door is always closed. The floor is perfumed earth. The walls are decorated with flowers and garlands, and a lamp burns all night long. But it was not this splendor that prompted Rāhula to take up his residence here. It was simply because the senior monks had told him to find quarters for himself, and because he respected his elders and longed to observe the rules of the Saṅgha.

Indeed, from time to time the senior monks used to test him. When they saw him coming they would throw down a hand-broom or a little dust and then ask who had thrown it down after Rāhula had come in. "Well, Rāhula came that way," would be the accusation, but Rāhula never said that he did not know about it. On the contrary, he used to remove the mess and humbly ask for forgiveness, and he would not leave until he was forgiven. This is how anxious he was to observe the rules. And it was solely this anxiety which made him take up his dwelling in the outhouse.

Now, one early morning the Master halted at the door of the outhouse and coughed "Ahem."

"Ahem," responded Rāhula.

"Who is there?" said the Buddha.

"It is I, Rāhula," was the reply. The young man came out and bowed low.

"Why are you sleeping here, Rāhula?"

"Because I had nowhere else to go. Up until now, sir, the senior monks have been very kind to me. But they are so afraid of committing an offense that they will not give me shelter any more. So I took up residence here, because I thought it was a spot where I would not come into contact with anybody else."

The Master thought to himself, "If they treat Rāhula like this, what will they do to other novices who join the Saṅgha?" His heart was moved. So, at an early hour he gathered the monks and asked the Captain of the Faith, "I suppose, Sāriputta, you know where Rāhula is now living."

"No, sir, I do not."

"Sāriputta, Rāhula was living in the outhouse. Sāriputta, if you treat Rāhula like this, how will you treat other youths who you admit to the Sangha? If you treat them like this they will not want to stay. In the future, keep your novices in your own hut for a day or two, and only let them find their own quarters on the third day, and take care to know where they are staying." With this new provision, the Master laid down the precept.

Gathering together in the Dharma hall, the monks spoke of the goodness of Rāhula. "See, sirs, how anxious Rāhula was to observe the rules. When told to find his own lodging, he did not say, 'I am the son of the Buddha. You get out!' No. He did not do this to a single monk. Instead he lived in the outhouse."

As they were talking about this, the Master came to the hall and took his seat saying, "What are you talking about, monks?"

"Sir," they replied, "we were talking of the determination of Rāhula to keep the rules."

Then the Master said, "Rāhula has not just shown this determination now. He also did this in the past when he was born as an animal." And he told this story of the past.

Once upon a time a certain king of Magadha was reigning in Rājagaha. In those days the Bodhisatta, having been born a buck, was living in the forest at the head of a herd of deer. Now his sister brought her son to him, saying, "Brother, teach your nephew the skills of deer." "Certainly," said the Bodhisatta. "Now go away, my boy, and come back at such and such a time and I will teach you." Punctually at the time his uncle mentioned, the young buck was there and he received instruction in the skills of deer.

One day as he was ranging the woods, he was caught in a trap, and he cried out. The herd ran away and told the mother that her son had been captured. She ran to her brother and asked him whether his nephew had been taught the skills of deer. "Do not be afraid. Your son is not at fault," said the Bodhisatta. "He has learned well the skills of deer, and he will come back to your great rejoicing." Having said this, he repeated this poem:

16: Tipallattha-miga Jātaka, The Cunning Deer

In all three postures - on his back or sides
Your son is versed. He's trained to use his hoofs.
And except at midnight never satisfies his thirst.
As he lies down on earth, he seems lifeless,
And only breathes with his under-nostril.
My nephew knows six tricks to cheat his foes.

Thus the Bodhisatta consoled his sister by showing her how thoroughly her son had mastered the skills of deer.

Meanwhile the young buck did not struggle in the trap. Rather he lay down on his side with his legs stretched out taut and rigid. He pawed up the ground around his hoofs to scatter the grass and earth. He let his head fall, rolled out his tongue; spit saliva all over his body, swelled himself up by breathing in deeply. He turned up his eyes, breathing only with the lower nostril, holding his breath with the upper one. He made himself so rigid and so stiff he looked like a corpse. Even the flies swarmed around him, and some crows flew overhead.

Figure: The Well-trained Young Buck

The hunter came up and smacked the buck on the belly with his hand, remarking, "He must have been caught early this morning. He's going bad already." The man untied the buck from his bonds and said to himself, "I'll cut him up here and take the flesh home with me." But as the man unsuspectingly went to gather sticks and leaves (to make a fire with), the young buck rose to his feet, shook himself, stretched out his neck, and, like a little cloud sailing before a mighty wind, sped swiftly back to his mother.

After repeating what he had said about Rāhula's having shown no less determination in time past to keep rules than in the present, the Master made the connection and identified the birth by saying, "Rāhula was the young stag of those days. Uppalavaṇṇā (*the nun*) his mother, and I was his uncle."

17: Māluta Jātaka,
In Light or Dark

This is a very simple but sweet story about how the Bodhisatta was able to solve a dispute between two friends and restore harmony to their relationship.

"*In light or dark.*" This story was told by the Master while at Jetavana. It is about two monks who had joined the Saṅgha in their old age. Tradition says that they were living in a hut in the forest in the Kosala country, and that one was named Elder Dark and the other Elder Light. Now one day Light said to Dark, "Sir, in what part of the month is it cold?"

"It is cold in the dark half of the month."

And one day Dark said to Light, "Sir, in what part of the month is it cold?"

"It is cold in the light half of the month."

As the two of them did not agree, they went to the Master and with due salutation asked, "Sir, in what part of the month is it cold?"

After the Master heard what they had to say, he said, "Monks, in bygone days also, I answered this same question for you. But your previous existences have become confused in your minds." (*For the monks, events in previous existences became jumbled together so that no distinct memory remained. A Buddha has the power of remembering the whole of his past existences.*) And so saying, he told this story of the past.

Once upon a time at the foot of a mountain, two friends, a lion and a tiger, were living together in the same cave. The Bodhisatta too was living at the foot of the same mountain as a hermit.

One day the two friends had a dispute about the cold. The tiger said it was cold in the dark half of the month, while the lion said that it was cold in the light half. As the two of them could not agree, they asked the Bodhisatta. He repeated this stanza:

> *In light or dark, whenever the wind blows,*
> *Then it is cold. For cold is caused by wind.*
> *And, therefore, I decide you both are right.*

In this way the Bodhisatta made peace between those friends.

Figure: The Lion, the Tiger, and the Hermit

When the Master had ended his lesson in support of what he had said as to his having answered the same question in bygone days, he preached the Four Noble Truths, after which both of the Elders won the Fruit of the First Path (*stream-entry*). The Master showed the connection and identified the birth, by saying, "Venerable Dark was the tiger of those days, Venerable Light the lion, and I myself the hermit who answered the question."

18: Matakabhatta Jātaka,
The Goat That Laughed and Cried

Animal sacrifice was common during the Buddha's time. This story is about the karmic consequences of killing. This teaching was so powerful that when India became a predominately Buddhist country in the first millennium, it also became a largely vegetarian country. This is true to this day.

"If people only knew." This story was told by the Master while at Jetavana. It is about Feasts for the Dead. For at this time people were killing goats, sheep, and other animals, and offering them up as a Feast for the Dead. They believed that this would benefit their dead relatives. Seeing what they were doing, the monks asked the Master, "Just now, sir, people are sacrificing many living creatures and offering them up as a Feast for the Dead. Can it be, sir, that there is any good in this?"

"No, monks," replied the Master. "No good arises when life is taken with the object of providing a Feast for the Dead. In bygone days wise people, preaching the Dharma from mid-air, showed the evil consequences of the practice. They made the whole continent renounce it. But now, when their previous existences have become confused in their minds, the practice has begun again." And, so saying, he told this story of the past.

Once upon a time when Brahmadatta was reigning in Benares, there was a brahmin who was well-versed in the Three Vedas. He was world-renowned as a teacher. He decided to offer a Feast for the Dead, so he obtained a goat and said to his pupils, "My sons, take this goat down to the river and bathe it. Then hang a garland round its neck, give it a pot of grain to eat, groom it, and bring it back."

"Very good," they said, and down to the river they took the goat. There they bathed and groomed the creature and set it on the bank. The goat, becoming conscious of the deeds of its past lives, was overjoyed at the thought that on this very day it would be freed from all its misery, and he laughed out loud. But then he thought that by killing him the brahmin would bear the misery of that misdeed. The goat felt a great compassion for the brahmin and began to cry. "Friend goat," said the young brahmins, "your voice has been loud both in laughter and in weeping. What made you laugh and what made you cry?"

"Ask me that question in front your master."

Figure: The Compassionate Goat

So they took the goat to their master and told him what happened. After hearing their story, the master asked the goat why it laughed and why it cried. Whereupon the animal, recalling its past deeds by its power to remember its former existences, said to the brahmin, "In the past, brahmin, I, like you, was a brahmin versed in the mystic texts of the Vedas. I, too, offered a Feast for the Dead, killing a goat for my offering. Because I killed that single goat, I have had my head cut off 500 times in 500 lives. This is my 500th and last birth to repay that debt. I laughed out loud when I thought that today I will finally be free from

18: Matakabhatta Jātaka,
The Goat That Laughed and Cried

my misery. But then I cried when I thought how today I will be freed from my misery, but you, as a penalty for killing me, would be doomed to lose your head, like me, 500 times. It was out of compassion for you that I cried."

"Do not be afraid, goat," said the brahmin. "I will not kill you."

"What do you say, brahmin?" said the goat. "Whether you kill me or not, I cannot escape death today."

"Fear not, goat. I will protect you."

"Your protection is weak, brahmin, and the power of my evil conduct is strong."

Setting the goat free, the brahmin said to his disciples, "Let us not allow anyone to kill this goat." And, accompanied by the young men, he stayed close to the animal. The moment the goat was set free, it reached out its neck to browse on the leaves of a bush growing near the top of a rock. At that very instant a thunderbolt struck the rock, shooting off pieces of rock that hit the goat on the outstretched neck and tore off its head. And people came and crowded around the dead goat.

In those days the Bodhisatta had been born a tree fairy in that same place. By his supernatural powers he now seated himself cross-legged in mid-air while all the crowd looked on. He thought to himself. "If these creatures only knew the results of this type if evil conduct, perhaps they would stop killing." In his sweet voice he taught them the Dharma in this stanza:

> If people but knew the penalty would be
> Birth into sorrow, living things would stop
> From taking life. Harsh is the killer's burden.

Thus did the Great Being preach the Dharma, scaring his hearers with the fear of hell. And the people, hearing him, were so terrified at the fear of hell that they stopped taking life. And the Bodhisatta, after teaching them in the Precepts and preaching the Dharma to them, passed away to fare according to his karma. The people, too, remained steadfast in the teaching of the Bodhisatta and spent their lives in charity and other good works, so that in the end they went the City of the Devas (*the heavenly realms*).

His lesson ended, the Master showed the connection, and identified the birth by saying, "In those days I was the tree fairy."

19: Āyācitabhatta Jātaka,
On Offerings Given

This is another warning tale about the dangers of killing animals. This one focuses on the consequences in the next life. Buddhist lore sometimes holds that fishermen are reborn as fish, and butchers are reborn as the animals they killed (!).

"*Consider your next life.*" This story was told by the Master while at Jetavana. It is about offering a sacrifice under vow to gods. Tradition says that in those days, when people went on a journey on business, they would sacrifice animals and offer them to the gods. Then they set off on their way after vowing, "If we come safely back with a profit, we will give you another sacrifice." And when they did come safely back with a profit, they believed that this was due to gods. This made them sacrifice many more animals in order to be released from their vow.

When the monks became aware of this, they asked the Blessed One, "Can there be any good in this, sir?"

The Blessed One told this story of the past.

Once upon a time in the Kāsi country, there was a fairy who lived in a banyan tree and stood at the entrance to a little village. A rich landowner from the village promised a sacrifice to the fairy if his business was profitable. Later, when this turned out to be so, he killed many animals and went to the tree to be released from his vow. But the tree fairy, standing in the fork of its tree, repeated this stanza:

> *Consider your life hereafter when you seek*
> *'Release,' for this release is strict bondage.*
> *This is not how the wise and good release themselves,*
> *For this, the fool's release ends in bondage.*

After that people refrained from taking life, and by walking in righteousness, they lived in the city of the Devas (*gods*) after death.

His lesson ended, the Master showed the connection, and identified the birth by saying, "In those days I was the tree fairy."

Jātaka Tales

Figure: The Rich Man and the Tree Fairy

20: Naḷapāna Jātaka,
The Monkey King and the Ogre

Another common theme in the Jātaka Tales is cleverness, an ability to solve problems creatively. This is a practical lesson for life. Now we would call it thinking outside the box, although the Bodhisatta had the advantage of magical powers!

"I found the footprints." The Master told this story while traveling on an alms pilgrimage through Kosala. He came to the village of Naḷakapāna (*bamboo drink*), and he was living at Ketakavana near the pool of Naḷakapāna. In those days the monks, after bathing in the pool of Naḷakapāna, made the novices get them bamboo for needle cases. (*In the Vinaya [Cv 5.11] the monks are allowed "the use of a needle case made of bamboo."*) But, seeing that they were hollow, they went to the Master and said, "Sir, we have bamboo with which to make needle cases, and from top to bottom they are hollow. How can that be?"

"Monks," said the Master, "I made this decree in times gone by." And, so saying, he told this story of the past.

In past times, we are told, there was a thick forest on this spot. And in the lake a water ogre lived. He would devour everyone who went down into the water. In those days the Bodhisatta had come to life as the king of the monkeys. He was as big as the fawn of a red deer. He lived in that forest at the head of a troop of no less than 80,000 monkeys who he protected. He counseled his subjects, "My friends, in this forest there are trees that are poisonous and lakes that are haunted by ogres. Always ask me first before you eat any fruit that you have not eaten before, or drink water where you have not drunk before."

"Certainly," they said.

One day they came to a spot they had never visited before. As, they were searching for water to drink after their day's wanderings, they came on this lake. But they did not drink. On the contrary, they sat down and waited for the Bodhisatta.

When he arrived, he said, "Well, my friends, why aren't you drinking?"

"We waited for you to come."

"Quite right, my friends," he said. Then he walked around the lake and looked for the footprints. When he did this he discovered that all the footprints led down into the water but none came back up. "Without doubt," he thought to himself, "this is the haunt of an ogre." So he said to his followers, "You are quite right, my friends, to not drink this water, for the lake is haunted by an ogre."

When the water ogre realized that they were not going to go into his lake, he assumed the shape of a horrible monster with a blue belly, a white face, and bright red hands and feet. Then he came out from the water, and said, "Why are you sitting here? Go down into the lake and drink." But the Bodhisatta said to him, "Aren't you the ogre of this water?"

"Yes, I am," the ogre replied.

"Do you kill all those who go down into this water?"

"Yes, I do, from small birds upwards. I never let anything go that comes down into my water. I will eat the lot of you too."

"But we will not let you eat us."

"Just drink the water."

"Yes, we will drink the water, and yet we will not fall into your power."

"How are you going to drink the water, then?"

"Ah, you think we will have to go down into the water to drink. But we will not enter the water at all. The whole 80,000 of us will take a bamboo stick and drink from your lake as easily as we could through the hollow stalk of a lotus. And so you will not be able to eat us." And he repeated the following stanza:

> I found the footprints all lead down, none back.
> With bamboo we'll drink; you shall not take my life.

So saying, the Bodhisatta had a stalk of bamboo brought to him. Then, calling to mind the Ten Perfections displayed by him, he recited them in a solemn declaration, and blew down the cane. Immediately the bamboo became hollow. In this way he had another and another bamboo stick brought to him and he blew down them. Next the Bodhisatta made the tour of the lake, and commanded, saying, "Let all bamboo growing here become hollow throughout." Now, thanks to

20: Naḷapāna Jātaka,
The Monkey King and the Ogre

the great virtues of the saving goodness of Bodhisattas, their commands are always fulfilled. And so every single piece of bamboo that grew round that lake became hollow.

Figure: The Wise Monkey King and the Angry Ogre

After giving this command, the Bodhisatta seated himself with a bamboo stick in his hands. All the other 80,000 monkeys also seated themselves round the lake, each with a piece of bamboo in his hands. And at the same moment when the Bodhisatta sucked the water up through his stick, they all drank too in the same manner. This was the way they drank, and the water ogre could not get any of them. He went into a rage. And the Bodhisatta went with his following back into the forest.

When the Master ended his lesson, he repeated what he had said about the hollowness of the bamboo being the result of a former decree of his. He showed the connection and identified the birth by saying, "Devadatta was the water ogre of those days. My disciples were the 80,000 monkeys, and I was the monkey king, so fertile in resource."

21: Kuruṅga Jātaka,
The Clever Antelope

Here we go again with Devadatta. I wonder if he had any idea that 2,500 years after he lived his name would still be known as the embodiment of wickedness and evil!

"The antelope knows well." This story was told by the Master while at the bamboo grove. It is about Devadatta. Once when the monks were gathered together in the Dharma Hall, they sat talking reproachfully of Devadatta, saying, "Sirs, with a view to destroy the Buddha Devadatta hired bowmen, hurled down a rock, and let loose the elephant Dhanapālaka. In every way possible he tries to kill the Lord of Wisdom." (*According to the Buddhist texts, Devadatta tried to kill the Buddha three times. The first time he hired mercenaries, the second time he tried to kill him by rolling a rock down a hill, and the third time he tried to let loose a drunken bull elephant. In this Jātaka the elephant is named Dhanapālaka; in the Vinaya account he is named Nāḷāgiri.*) Entering and seating himself on the seat prepared for him, the Master asked, "Sirs, what were you discussing?"

"Sir," they replied, "we were discussing the wickedness of Devadatta, saying that he is always trying to kill you."

The Master said, "It is not only in these present days, monks, that Devadatta tries to kill me. He did the same thing in bygone days also. However, then as now, he was unsuccessful." And so saying, he told this story of the past.

Once upon a time when Brahmadatta was king of Benares, the Bodhisatta was born as an antelope, and he used to live on fruits in his haunts in the forest.

At one time he was eating the fruit of a sepaṇṇi tree. (*A sepaṇṇi tree is any tree that grows fruit that animals will eat.*) And there was a village hunter, whose technique was to build a platform in a tree where he found the track of deer and to wait for them to come eat the fruit. When the deer came, he shot them down with an arrow and sold the flesh for a living. One day this hunter saw the tracks of the Bodhisatta at the foot of the tree and made a platform up in that tree. Having breakfasted early, he went with his bow into the forest and climbed

21: Kuruṅga Jātaka,
The Clever Antelope

up onto his platform. The Bodhisatta, too, came early to eat the fruit of that tree. But he was not in too great a hurry to approach it. He thought to himself, "Sometimes these hunters build a platform for themselves in the tree limbs. Is it possible that this has happened here?" He stopped some way off to observe. Finding that the Bodhisatta did not approach, the hunter, still seated on his platform, threw fruit down in front of the antelope. The antelope said to himself, "Here's the fruit coming down to me. I wonder if there is a hunter up there." So he looked more closely until he saw the hunter in the tree. But pretending not to see the man, he shouted, "My worthy tree, in the past you have let your fruit fall straight to the ground, but today you have stopped acting like a tree. And since you have stopped to act like a tree, I, too, must change, and look for food somewhere else." Having said this, he repeated this stanza:

The antelope knows well the fruit you drop.
I do not like it; I will find some other tree.

Figure: The Clever Antelope and the Angry Hunter

Then the hunter shot his arrow at the Bodhisatta, crying, "Begone! I've missed you this time." Spinning around, the Bodhisatta halted and said, "You may have missed me, my good man; but depend upon it, you will not miss the results of your conduct. That is to say the eight large and the sixteen lesser hells and the five forms of bondage and torture." With these words the antelope bounded off on its way, and the hunter, too, climbed down and went his way.

When the Master ended this discourse and repeated what he had said about Devadatta's going about to kill him in bygone days, he showed the connection and identified the birth, by saying, "Devadatta was the hunter of those days, and I was the antelope."

22: Kukkura Jātaka,
The Dog's Teaching

This is another story in which the result of the Bodhisatta's wisdom and compassion is that animals – in this case dogs – were protected from harm for "10,000 years." For someone who grew up listening to these stories, it created a culture of kindness and compassion towards animals. By the time of King Ashoka - about 200 years after the Buddha died - this led to widespread vegetarianism in India as well as universal healthcare for animals. The descendants of those Ashokan veterinary clinics still exist in some places today.

"The dogs that grow in the royal palace." This story was told by the Master while at Jetavana. It is about acting for the good of kinsfolk, as is also told in the Bhaddasāla Jātaka (*Jātaka 465*). It was to drive home this lesson that he told this story of the past.

Once upon a time when Brahmadatta was reigning in Benares, the Bodhisatta was reborn as a dog because of his past karma, and he lived in a great cemetery as the leader of several hundred dogs.

Now one day the King set out for his pleasure garden in his chariot of state drawn by milk-white horses. After amusing himself all day in the grounds, he came back to the city after sunset. They left the carriage harness in the courtyard still hitched on to the chariot. During the night it rained and the harness got wet. In addition, the King's dogs came down from the upper chambers and gnawed the leather work and straps.

The next day they told the King, "Sire, dogs have got in through the mouth of the sewer and have gnawed the leather work and straps of your majesty's carriage." Enraged at the dogs the King said, "Kill every dog you see."

They began a great slaughter of dogs. The poor creatures, finding that they were being killed whenever they were seen, retreated to the refuge of the cemetery. The Bodhisatta asked them, "What is the meaning of this? Why are all of you gathering here?" They said, "The King is so angry that the leather work and straps of his carriage have been gnawed by dogs that he ordered all dogs to be killed. Dogs are being destroyed wholesale, and there is great danger."

The Bodhisatta thought to himself, "No dogs can get into the palace because it is so closely watched. It must be the thoroughbred dogs inside the palace who have done it. Nothing is happening to the real culprits, while the guiltless are being put to death. What if I were to show the King who the real culprits are and save the lives of my kith and kin?" He comforted his kinsfolk by saying, "Have no fear. I will save you. Just wait here until I see the King."

Guided by thoughts of loving-kindness and calling to mind the Ten Perfections, he went into the city alone and unattended, commanding, "Let no hand be lifted to throw sticks or stones at me." Accordingly, when he made his appearance, no one grew angry when they saw him.

The King, meantime, after ordering the dogs' destruction, took his seat in the hall of justice. The Bodhisatta ran straight to him, leaping under the King's throne. The King's servants tried to get him out but his majesty stopped them. Taking heart a little, the Bodhisatta came out from under the throne. He bowed to the King and said, "Is it you who ordered the dogs destroyed?"

"Yes, it is me."

"What is their offense, King of men?"

"They have been gnawing the straps and the leather covering my carriage."

"Do you know the dogs who actually did the mischief?"

"No, I do not."

"But, your majesty, if you do not know for certain the real culprits, it is not right to order the destruction of every dog that is seen."

"It was because dogs gnawed the leather of my carriage that I ordered them all to be killed."

"Do your people kill all dogs without exception, or are there some dogs who are spared?"

"Some are spared - the thoroughbred dogs of my own palace."

"Sire, just now you said that you ordered the universal slaughter of all dogs wherever they are found because dogs gnawed the leather of your carriage. But now you say that the thoroughbred dogs of your own palace escape death. Therefore you are following the four Evil

22: Kukkura Jātaka,
The Dog's Teaching

Courses of partiality, dislike, ignorance, and fear. Such courses are wrong and not kinglike. When dispensing justice kings should be as unbiased as the beam of a balance. But in this instance, since the royal dogs go free while poor dogs are killed, this is not the impartial doom of all dogs alike. It is only the slaughter of poor dogs."

And then the Great Being, lifting up his sweet voice, said, "Sire, it is not justice that you are performing," and he taught the Dharma to the King in this stanza:

> *The dogs that live in the royal palace,*
> *The well-bred dogs, so strong and fair of form,*
> *Not these, but only we, are doomed to die.*
> *There's no impartial sentence given out*
> *To all alike; it is slaughter of the poor.*

After listening to the Bodhisatta's words, the King said, "In your wisdom do you know who actually gnawed the leather of my carriage?"

"Yes, sire."

"Who was it?"

"The thoroughbred dogs that live in your own palace."

"Can you prove that they were the ones who gnawed the leather?"

"I can."

"Do so, wise one."

"Then send for your dogs and have a little buttermilk and kusa grass brought in."

The King did so.

Then the Great Being said, "Mash this grass up in the buttermilk and make the dogs drink it."

The King did so with the result that each dog, as he drank, vomited. And up came bits of leather!

"Why it is like a judgment of a Perfect Buddha himself," cried the overjoyed King, and he did homage to the Bodhisatta by offering him the royal umbrella (*the white umbrella which is the symbol of royal authority*). Instead the Bodhisatta taught the Dharma in the ten stanzas on righteousness in the Tesakuṇa Jātaka (*Jātaka 521*), beginning with the words:

Walk righteously, great King of princely race.

Figure: The King and the Wise Dog

Then having established the King in the Five Precepts, and having exhorted his majesty to be steadfast, the Bodhisatta handed the white umbrella of kingship back to the King.

At the close of the Great Being's words, the King commanded that the lives of all creatures should be safe from harm. He ordered that all dogs from the Bodhisatta downwards should have a constant supply of the same food that he ate. And, abiding by the teachings of the Bodhisatta, he spent his life in charity and good deeds. When he died he was reborn in the Deva Heaven. The "Dog's Teaching" endured for ten thousand years. The Bodhisatta also lived to a ripe old age and then passed away to fare according to his karma.

22: Kukkura Jātaka, The Dog's Teaching

When the Master ended this lesson, he said, "Not only now, monks, does the Buddha do what benefits his kindred. In former times he also did this." He showed the connection and identified the birth by saying, "Ānanda was the King of those days. The Buddha's followers were the others, and I myself was the dog."

23: Bhojājānīya Jātaka, *The War Horse*

This is a tale of mercy as well as political practicality. After being attacked by seven kings, the King of Benares could have exacted revenge. Instead, after being advised by the Bodhisatta, he treated them charitably. This was not only compassionate and humane, it led to them into never attacking him again, and the kingdoms were able to live peacefully together.

We have an example in more modern history. After World War I, the Treaty of Versailles exacted brutal revenge on the Germans. This led to a great deal of suffering in post-war Germany. In turn this led to the rise of fascism and World War II. After World War II, however, the Marshal Plan helped reconstruct Europe and Japan, leading to many decades of peace, and to Germany and Japan becoming two of the more stable countries in the world.

"Though prostrate now." This story was told by the Master while at Jetavana. It is about a monk who gave up persevering. For it was then that the Master addressed that monk and said, "Monks, in bygone days the wise and good persevered even amid hostile surroundings, and even when they were wounded, they still did not give in." And, so saying, he told this story of the past.

Once upon a time when Brahmadatta was reigning in Benares, the Bodhisatta was born as a thoroughbred horse and was made the King's personal war horse, surrounded by pomp and pageantry. He ate exquisite three-year old rice that was served to him in a golden dish worth a hundred thousand pieces of money. The ground of his stall was perfumed. Around his stall there were crimson curtains, while overhead there was a canopy studded with stars of gold. The walls were decorated with wreaths and garlands of fragrant flowers, and a lamp fed with scented oil was always burning there.

All the kings around Benares coveted the kingdom. Once seven kings surrounded Benares and sent an ultimatum to the King, saying, "Either give up your kingdom to us or we will attack." Assembling his ministers, the King of Benares put the matter before them and asked them what to do. They said, "First of all, you should not go into battle yourself. Send your best cavalryman out to fight them. If he fails, we will decide what to do next."

23: Bhojājānīya Jātaka,
The War Horse

Then the King sent for that cavalryman and said to him, "Can you fight the seven kings, my dear soldier?" He said, "Give me your noble war horse, and then I could not only fight those seven kings, I could defeat all the kings in India."

"My dear soldier, take my war horse or any other horse you want and do battle."

"Very good, my sovereign lord," said the cavalryman, and with a bow he passed down from the upper chambers of the palace. Then he had the noble war horse led out and sheathed in armor, armoring himself as well from head to toe. Strapping on his sword, he mounted on his noble steed and passed out of the city gate. Then, with a lightning charge, he broke down the first camp, taking one king alive and bringing him back as a prisoner into the soldiers' custody.

Returning to the field, he broke down the second and the third camps, and so on until he captured five kings, all alive. The sixth camp he broke down and captured the sixth king. But his war horse was wounded. He streamed with blood and the noble animal suffered from sharp pain. Seeing that the horse was wounded, the cavalryman had it lie down at the King's gate. He loosened its armor and started to armor another horse.

As the Bodhisatta lay at full length on his side, he opened his eyes and saw what the cavalryman was doing. "My rider," he thought to himself, "is putting armor on another horse. That other horse will never be able to break down the seventh camp and capture the seventh king. He will lose all that I have accomplished. This brave cavalryman will be killed, and the King will fall into the hands of the enemy. I alone, and no other horse, can break down that seventh camp and capture the seventh king."

So, as he lay there, he called to the cavalryman and said, "Sir, there is no horse who can break down the seventh camp and capture the seventh king. I will not throw away what I have already done. Help me get up on my feet and put on my armor again." And so saying, he repeated this stanza:

> *Though lying now, and pierced with arrows,*
> *Yet still no one can match the war horse.*
> *So harness none but me, O charioteer.*

The cavalryman helped the Bodhisatta get up on his feet, bound his wound, and put his armor on him again. Mounted on the war horse, he broke down the seventh camp and brought back the seventh king alive. He handed him over to the custody of the soldiers.

They led the Bodhisatta up to the King's gate, and the King came out to look at him. Then the Great Being said to the King, "Great King, do not kill these seven kings. Have them swear a loyalty oath to you and let them go. Let the cavalryman enjoy all the honor due to us both, for it is not right that a warrior who has presented you with seven captive kings should not be honored. And as for yourself, exercise charity, keep the Precepts, and rule your kingdom in righteousness and justice." When the Bodhisatta had thus exhorted the King, they started to take off his armor. But as they were taking it off, he died.

Figure: The War Horse Addresses the King

The King had the body cremated with all respect, and he bestowed great honor on the cavalryman. He sent the seven kings to their homes after having them swear an oath never to war against him again. And he ruled his kingdom in righteousness and justice, passing away when his life ended to fare according to his karma.

23: Bhojājānīya Jātaka,
The War Horse

Then the Master said, "Thus, monks, in bygone days the wise and good persevered even amid hostile surroundings. Even when wounded so grievously, I still did not give in. Whereas you who have devoted yourself to practicing the Dharma, why do you give up so easily?" Then he preached the Four Noble Truths, after which the faint-hearted monk won Arahatship. His lesson ended, the Master showed the connection. He identified the birth by saying, "Ānanda was the King of those days, Sāriputta the cavalryman, and I was the war horse." (*Sāriputta was one of the Buddha's two chief disciples.*)

24: Ājañña Jātaka,
The Thoroughbred War Horse

It is noteworthy that so many of these stories are about encouraging people not to give up on following the path. Modern day meditators probably sympathize with how discouraging it can be to put in so much effort and yet feel like you are not getting anywhere.

Ṭhānissaro Bhikkhu says that once he went back through his teacher Ajahn Lee's discourses, and 80% of them were words of encouragement. Then as now, attaining awakening is not easy.

"No matter when or where." This story was told by the Master while at Jetavana. It is about another monk who gave up persevering. But, in this case, he addressed that monk and said, "Monk, in bygone days the wise and good still persevered even when wounded." And, so saying, he told this story of the past.

Once upon a time when Brahmadatta was reigning in Benares, there were seven kings who surrounded the city, just as in the previous story.

So a warrior who fought from a chariot harnessed two thoroughbred horses who were brothers. He left the city, broke down six of the camps, and captured six kings. But in the sixth sortie, the elder horse was wounded. The charioteer drove on until he reached the King's gate, where he took the elder brother out of the chariot. After unfastening the horse's armor as he lay upon one side, he started to put armor on another horse. Realizing the warrior's intent, the Bodhisatta had the same thoughts pass through his head as in the foregoing story. He sent for the charioteer, and repeated this stanza as he lay:

> *No matter when or where, wounded or distressed,*
> *The thoroughbred fights on; the weak give in.*

The charioteer had the Bodhisatta set on his feet and harnessed. Then he broke down the seventh camp and took the seventh king prisoner. He drove to the King's gate, and there took out the noble horse. As he lay upon one side, the Bodhisatta gave the same advice to the King as in the previous story, and then he died. The King had the body

24: Ājañña Jātaka,
The Thoroughbred War Horse

cremated with all respect. He lavished honor on the charioteer, and after ruling his kingdom in righteousness, he passed away to fare according to his karma.

Figure: The Cavalryman and the Wounded War Horse

His lesson ended, the Master taught the Four Noble Truths, after which that monk won Arahatship. He identified the birth by saying, "The Elder Ānanda was the King, and the Perfect Buddha was the horse of those days."

25: Tittha Jātaka, *The Horse at the Ford*

There is a subtle point to make in stories like this one. Some schools of Buddhism say that only a guru can "impart transcendent knowledge." But you will not find this in the Buddha's teachings. Even a Buddha is only a guide. You must make the journey. A wise teacher can help create the conditions for awakening, but only the dedicated student can attain awakening by his or her own effort and skill. A teacher is like a coach; a student is like the athlete.

There is, however, an error in this story. It says that only a Buddha can know the hearts and minds of others. While I would not say it is common, the ability to read minds is known even among non-Buddhists. This was probably added to make the Buddha seem even more remarkable.

"*Change the spot.*" This story was told by the Master while at Jetavana. It is about an ex-goldsmith who had become a monk and was living as a companion with the Guardian of the Faith (*Sāriputta*).

Now, only a Buddha knows the hearts and minds of others. Because he lacked this power, the Guardian of the Faith told his companion to use impurity as the theme for his meditation. This was not an appropriate them for meditation for that monk. The reason why it was no good to him was that, according to tradition, he had been born for 500 consecutive births as a goldsmith. The cumulative effect of seeing absolutely pure gold for so long had made the theme of impurity useless. He spent four months without making the slightest progress in his meditation. Finding himself unable to help his companion, the Guardian of the Faith thought to himself, "This must be someone that only a Buddha can teach. I will take him to the Buddha." So at early dawn he took the monk to the Master.

The Master said, "What has brought you, Sāriputta, here with this monk?"

"Sir, I gave him a theme for meditation, and after four months he has not made even the slightest progress. So I brought him to you thinking that he is someone that only a Buddha can teach."

"What meditation, Sāriputta, did you prescribe for him?"

"The meditation on impurity, Blessed One."

25: Tittha Jātaka,
The Horse at the Ford

"Sāriputta, you do not have the power to know the hearts and minds of others. Leave us and come back in the evening to get your companion."

After the Elder left, the Master had the monk change into a nice undercloth and a robe. He kept him at his side when he went into town for alms, and he made sure that he received the best food. That evening, as he walked around the monastery with that monk by his side, he made a pond appear. A great clump of lotuses grew in it, and there was one particularly large and beautiful lotus flower. "Sit here, brother," he said, "and look at this flower." And leaving the monk, he went back to his perfumed chamber.

That monk gazed and gazed at that flower. The Blessed One made it slowly decay. So as the monk looked at it, the flower began to fade. The petals fell off, beginning at the rim, until they were all gone. Then the stamens fell away, and only the pod was left. As he watched the monk thought to himself, "This lotus flower was lovely and fair. Yet now its color is gone and only the pod is left standing. Just as this lotus has decayed, this will happen to my body. All compounded things are subject to change. They are inconstant and impermanent!" And with that thought he attained his first insight.

Knowing that the monk's mind had attained this insight, the Master, seated as he was in his perfumed chamber, projected a radiant image of himself and uttered this stanza:

> Pluck out conceit, just as you would pluck
> The autumn water lily. Set your heart
> On nothing but this, the perfect Path of Peace,
> And that end to suffering that the Buddha taught.

At the close of this stanza, that monk won Arahatship. At the thought that he would never be born again, never be troubled with existence ever again, he burst into a heartfelt utterance beginning with these stanzas. He who has lived his life, whose thought is ripe:

> He who is purged and free from all defilements,
> Wears his last body; he whose life is pure,
> Reigns over his senses as a sovereign lord,
> He, like the moon that wins her way at last
> From Rāhu's jaws, has won supreme release.

*The foulness which enveloped me, which brought
Delusion's utter darkness, I dispelled;
As the beaming sun with a thousand rays
Lights up heaven with a flood of light.*

(*Rāhu was a kind of Titan who was thought to cause eclipses by temporarily swallowing the sun and moon.*)

After this and with renewed utterances of joy, he went to the Blessed One and saluted him. The Elder, too, came, and after due salutation to the Master went away with his companion.

When news of all this spread among the Saṅgha, they gathered together in the Dharma Hall and praised the virtues of the Lord of Wisdom, saying, "Sirs, by not knowing the hearts and thoughts of men, the Elder Sāriputta was ignorant of his companion's disposition. But the Master knew, and in a single day our brother was able to attain Arahatship. Oh, the marvelous powers of a Buddha are great!"

Entering and taking the seat set ready for him, the Master asked, "What are you talking about, brothers?"

"Nothing else, Blessed One, then this: that you alone knew the heart and the thoughts of the companion of the Captain of the Faith."

"This is no marvel, brothers, that I, as Buddha, should now that monk's disposition. Even in bygone days I knew it." And, so saying, he told this story of the past.

Once upon a time Brahmadatta was reigning in Benares. In those days the Bodhisatta used to be the King's minister in things both worldly and spiritual. At this time some people had washed a horse, a sorry beast, at the bathing place of the King's war horse. And when the groom led the war horse down to the same water, the animal was so insulted that he would not go in. So the groom went off to the King and said, "Please your Majesty, your war horse will not take his bath."

Then the King sent the Bodhisatta, saying, "Go, wise one, and find out why the animal will not go into the water."

"Very good, sire," said the Bodhisatta, and he went down to the waterside. There he examined the horse, and, finding it was not sick, he tried to determine what the reason was. At last he understood that some other horse must have been washed there, and that the war horse

25: Tittha Jātaka, The Horse at the Ford

had been so insulted that he would not go into the water. So he asked the grooms what animal they had washed first in the water. "Another horse, my lord. It was an ordinary animal."

Figure: The Reluctant (and Snobby!) Horse

"Ah, his arrogance has caused him to be so offended that he will not go into the water," the Bodhisatta said to himself. "The thing to do is to wash him somewhere else." So he said to the groom, "A man gets tired, my friend, of even the best food if he has it all the time. And that's how this horse is. He has been washed here so many times. Take him somewhere else and bathe him there." And so saying, he repeated this stanza:

> *Change the spot, and let the war horse bathe*
> *Now here, now there, with a constant change of scene.*
> *For even the finest food bores a man at last.*

After listening to his words, they led the horse off elsewhere, and watered and bathed him. And while they were washing the animal down afterwards, the Bodhisatta went back to the King. "Well," said the King, "has my horse been watered and bathed, my friend?"

"He has, sire."

"Why wouldn't he do it before?"

"For the following reason," said the Bodhisatta, and he told the King the whole story. "What a clever fellow he is," said the King. "He can read even read the mind of an animal." And he gave great honor to the Bodhisatta, and when his life ended he passed away to fare according to his karma. The Bodhisatta also passed away to fare likewise according to his karma.

When the Master ended his lesson and had repeated what he had said about his knowledge, in the past as well as the present, of that monk's disposition, he showed the connection. He identified the birth by saying, "This monk was the war horse of those days. Ānanda was the King, and I was the wise minister."

26: Mahilāmukha Jātaka, *The Elephant Damsel-face*

In the following story, note that Prince Ajātasattu was the son of King Bimbisara, the King of Magadha. King Bimbisara was a good man and a loyal follower of the Buddha. However, Devadatta conspired with Prince Ajātasattu to kill King Bimbisara and the Buddha, so that Ajātasattu would be become King and Devadatta would become the leader of the Saṇgha. At the time of this story Ajātasattu is apparently not yet the King. It is not clear if the story happens before, during, or after Devadatta's attempts to kill the Buddha.

There are many stories like this in the Canon about monks (I have not seen one – yet – about a nun, but I am sure they exist!) trying to bend the rules. Some things never change, and stories like this show how the human mind has not changed in 2500 years.

"*Through hearing first.*" This story was told by the Master while at the bamboo grove. It is about Devadatta, who attained both gain and honor because of the support of Prince Ajātasattu. Prince Ajātasattu built a monastery for Devadatta at Gayāsīsa. Every day he brought him five hundred kettles of perfumed three-year-old rice that was seasoned with all the best spices. All this gain and honor brought Devadatta many followers. Devadatta lived with them without ever leaving his monastery.

At that time there were two friends living in Rājagaha. One of whom took his vows under the Master, while the other took them under Devadatta. They continued to see each other, either casually or by visiting the monasteries. One day the disciple of Devadatta said to the other, "Sir, why do you go on daily alms rounds when they cause you such strain? Devadatta sits quietly at Gayāsīsa and feeds on the best food, seasoned with all the best spices. There's no way like his. Why create misery for yourself? Why don't you come in the morning to the monastery at Gayāsīsa and drink our sweet milk, try our eighteen kinds of solid food, and enjoy our excellent fare that is seasoned with all the best spices?"

Being pressured over and over again to accept the invitation, the Buddha's monk began to want to go, and finally he began to go to

Gayāsīsa, where he ate and ate. However, he always returned to the Bamboo grove at the proper hour.

It was not possible to hide forever what he was doing, and after a while it came out that he was going to Gayāsīsa and delighting himself with the food provided for Devadatta. His friends asked him, "Is it true, as they say, that you delight yourself on the food provided for Devadatta?"

"Who said that?" he said.

"So-and-so said it."

"It is true, sirs, that I go to Gayāsīsa and eat there. But it is not Devadatta who gives me food. Others do that."

"Sir, Devadatta is the enemy of the Buddhas. In his wickedness, he has gotten the support of Ajātasattu, and by that wickedness gotten gain and honor for himself. Yet you who took the vows according to this faith that leads to salvation, you eat the food that Devadatta gets by wickedness. Come. Let us take you to the Master." And, taking the monk with them, they went to the Dharma Hall.

When the Master became aware of their presence, he said, "Monks, are you bringing this monk here against his will?"

"Yes, sir. This monk, after taking the vows with you, eats the food that Devadatta gets by his wickedness."

"Is it true, as they say, that you eat the food that Devadatta gets by wickedness?"

"It was not Devadatta, sir, that gave it to me, but others."

"Do not quibble here, monk," the Master said. "Devadatta is a man of bad conduct and bad principle. Oh, how could you, who have taken the vows here, eat Devadatta's food while practicing my Dharma? But you have always been prone to going astray and have followed anyone you meet." And, so saying, he told this story of the past.

Once upon a time when Brahmadatta was reigning in Benares, the Bodhisatta became his minister. In those days the King had a state elephant named Damsel-face. He was virtuous and good and never hurt anyone.

26: Mahilāmukha Jātaka,
The Elephant Damsel-face

Now one day some burglars came near the elephant's stall at night and sat down to discuss their plans to commit a robbery in these words: "This is the way to tunnel into a house. This is the way to break in through the walls. Before carrying off the plunder, the tunnel or breach in the walls should be made as clear and open as a road or a ford. When stealing the goods, you shouldn't be reluctant to kill. Otherwise there may be those who try to stop us. A burglar should get rid of any sense of shame and be pitiless, a man of cruelty and violence."

After having agreed to act in this evil way, the burglars left. The next day they came again, and many other days as well, and they had similar conversations. Finally the elephant decided that they had come to teach him, and that he must become pitiless, cruel, and violent. And so it happened. No sooner did his mahout (*elephant handler*) appear in the early morning than the elephant took the man in his trunk and threw him to the ground and killed him. He did the same thing to a second, and a third, and to every person who came near him.

Figure: The Wicked Elephant

The news was brought to the King that Damsel-face had gone mad and was killing everybody that he saw. So the King sent the Bodhisatta, saying, "Go, wise man, and find out what has happened to him."

Away went the Bodhisatta, and he soon satisfied himself that the elephant was not sick. As he thought over the possible causes of the change, he decided that the elephant must have heard people talking near him and imagined that they were giving him a lesson, and that this was what had corrupted the animal. Accordingly, he asked the elephant handlers whether anyone had been talking together recently near the stall. "Yes, my lord," they answered. "Some burglars came and talked." Then the Bodhisatta went and told the King, saying, "There is nothing wrong, sire, with the elephant physically. He has been corrupted by overhearing some burglars talk."

"Well, what should we do?"

"Order good men, sages and brahmins, to sit in his stall and talk about virtuous conduct."

"Do so, my friend," said the King.

Then the Bodhisatta sent good men, sages and brahmins, to the stall, and he told them to discuss virtuous conduct. Sitting down near the elephant, they spoke as follows, "You should never cause harm or kill. All good beings should be compassionate, loving, and merciful."

Hearing this the elephant thought they must mean this as a lesson for him, and he resolved to become good. And so it happened that he became good again.

"Well, my friend," said the King to the Bodhisatta, "is he well now?"

"Yes, your majesty," said the Bodhisatta. "Thanks to wise and good men, the corrupted elephant has become himself again." And so saying, he repeated this stanza:

Through hearing first the burglars' wicked talk
Damsel-face ranged abroad to wound and kill.
Through hearing later wise men's virtuous words
The noble elephant became good once again.

26: Mahilāmukha Jātaka,
The Elephant Damsel-face

The King said, "He can read the mind even of an animal!" And he bestowed great honor on the Bodhisatta. After living to a ripe old age, he, with the Bodhisatta, passed away to fare according to his karma.

The Master said, "In the past, too, you followed everyone you met, monk. Hearing burglars talk, you followed what they said, and hearing the wise and good talk, you followed what they said." His lesson ended, he showed the connection and identified the birth by saying, "The unfaithful monk was the Damsel-face of those days, Ānanda was the King, and I myself was the minister."

27: Abiṇha Jātaka,
The Elephant and the Dog

This is a lovely story about friendship. As the Buddha famously said:

"This is the entire holy life, Ānanda, that is, good friendship, good companionship, good comradeship. When a bhikkhu has a good friend, a good companion, a good comrade, it is to be expected that he will develop and cultivate the Noble Eightfold Path." - [SN 45.2]

Animals of different species often bind. The famous racehorse Seabiscuit had three close companions: a horse named Pumpkin, a dog named Pocatell, and a spider monkey named Jo-Jo.

"No morsel can he eat." This story was told by the Master while at Jetavana. It is about a lay disciple and an aged senior monk.

Tradition says that there were two friends in Sāvatthi, one of whom joined the Saṅgha. He used to go to the other's house every day where his friend gave him alms food. He would also make a meal for himself, and then accompany the monk back to the monastery. There he sat talking with his friend all day long until the sun went down, after which he went back to town. And his friend the monk escorted him home, going as far as the city gates before turning back.

The close friendship of these two became known among the Saṅgha. They were sitting one day in the Dharma Hall talking about the intimacy that existed between the pair when the Master entered the Hall. He asked what they were discussing, and the monks told him.

"Not only, monks, are these two close friends now," said the Master. "They were good friends in bygone days as well." And, so saying, he told this story of the past.

Once upon a time when Brahmadatta was reigning in Benares, the Bodhisatta became his minister. In those days there was a dog that used to go to the stall of the elephant of state and eat the rice that fell where the elephant fed. Visiting the place for the food's sake, the dog grew very friendly with the elephant, until eventually he would never eat except with him. Neither could get on without the other. The dog used to swing back and forth on the elephant's trunk. Now one day a villager bought the dog and took the dog home with him. After that

27: Abiṇha Jātaka,
The Elephant and the Dog

the elephant, missing the dog, refused either to eat or drink or take his bath, and the King was told about this. His majesty sent the Bodhisatta to find out why the elephant was acting like this. Going to the elephant house, the Bodhisatta, seeing how sad the elephant was, said to himself, "He is not physically ill. He must have formed an ardent friendship and is sad at the loss of his friend." So he asked whether the elephant had become friends with anyone.

"Yes, my lord," the elephant answered. "There's a very warm friendship between me and a dog."

"Where is that dog now?"

"A man took him."

"Do you know where that man lives?"

"No, my lord."

The Bodhisatta went to the King and said, "There is nothing physically wrong with the elephant, sire, but he was very friendly with a dog. It is missing his friend that has made him refuse to eat." And so saying, he repeated this stanza:

> *No morsel can he eat, no rice or grass.*
> *And in the bath he takes no pleasure now.*
> *I think the dog had grown so familiar,*
> *That elephant and dog were closest friends.*

"Well," said the King on hearing this, "what should we do, sage?"

"Make a proclamation by the beat of the drum, your majesty, that a man is reported to have carried off a dog of which the elephant of state was fond. And whoever has the dog will pay a fine."

The King acted on this advice. And the man, as soon as he heard of this, promptly let the dog loose. The dog ran away at once and made his way back to the elephant. The elephant took the dog up in his trunk and placed it on his head. He wept and cried, and, setting the dog back on the ground, made the dog eat first before he ate his own food.

"Even the minds of animals are known to him," said the King, and he loaded the Bodhisatta with honors.

The Master ended his lesson that showed that the two were intimate in bygone days as well as now. This done, he taught the Four Noble Truths. Then he showed the connection and identified the birth by saying, "The lay disciple was the dog of those days, the aged senior monk was the elephant, and I myself the wise minister."

Figure: The Joyful Friends Reunited

28: Nandivisāla Jātaka,
The Bull Who Won the Bet

The subject of proper speech is a constant theme in the Buddha's teachings. He gives a great deal of advice on what is proper to say and when it is the right time to say it. We probably do more harm with our careless speech than with anything else we do. It is a difficult skill to master, and it is one that requires constant attention.

"*Speak only words of kindness.*" The Master told this story at Jetavana. It is about harsh words spoken by the Six (*a group of six monks who were notorious for constantly breaking the monastic rules*). For in those days the Six, when they disagreed with respectable monks, used to taunt, revile and jeer them, and torment them with abuse. The monks reported this to the Blessed One, who sent for the Six and asked them whether this charge was true. On their admitting its truth, he rebuked them, saying, "Monks, harsh words offend even animals. In bygone days an animal caused a man who used harsh language to lose a thousand gold coins." And, so saying, he told this story of the past.

Once upon a time at Takkasilā in the land of Gandhāra there was a king reigning there, and the Bodhisatta was born as a bull. When he was quite a tiny calf, he was presented to a brahmin by his owners. They were known to give presents of oxen to holy men. The brahmin called it Nandi Visāla (Great Joy), and he treated it like his own child. He fed the young bull on rice pudding and fine rice. When the Bodhisatta grew up, he thought to himself, "I have been brought up by this brahmin with great care, and there is not another bull in all India that is as strong as I am. Perhaps I could repay the brahmin by a show of my strength." Accordingly, one day he said to the brahmin, "Go, brahmin, to some merchant who is rich in herds and bet a thousand gold pieces that your bull can draw a hundred loaded carts."

The brahmin found such a merchant and got into a discussion with him as to whose oxen in town were the strongest. "Oh, so-and-so's, or so-and-so's," said the merchant. "But," he added, "there are no oxen in the town that can compare with mine for real strength."

The brahmin replied, "I have a bull who can pull a hundred loaded carts."

"Where is such a bull to be found?" laughed the merchant.

"I've got him at home," said the brahmin.

"Make it a bet."

"Certainly," said the brahmin, and he bet a thousand gold pieces.

Then he loaded a hundred carts with sand, gravel, and stones, and leashed the lot together, one behind the other, by cords from the axle of the one in front to the one behind it. Then he bathed Nandi Visāla, gave him a measure of perfumed rice to eat, hung a garland round his neck, and harnessed him to the leading cart. The brahmin sat on the pole, and waved his whip in the air, shouting, "Now then, you scoundrel! Pull them along, you scoundrel!"

"I'm not a scoundrel," thought the Bodhisatta, and so he planted his four feet like so many posts and did not budge an inch.

The merchant made the brahmin pay the thousand gold pieces. His money gone, the brahmin took his bull and went home. There he lay down on his bed in agony and grief. When Nandi Visāla walked in and found the brahmin in such grief, he went up to him and asked if the brahmin were taking a nap. "How could I take a nap when I have lost a thousand gold pieces?!"

"Brahmin, in all the time that I have lived in your house, have I ever broken a pot, or squeezed up against anybody, or made a mess?"

"Never, my child."

"Then, why did you call me a scoundrel? It's you who are to blame, not me. Go and bet him two thousand gold pieces this time. Only do not call me scoundrel again."

When he heard this, the brahmin went off to the merchant and bet two thousand gold pieces. Just as before, he leashed the hundred carts to one another and harnessed Nandi Visāla, very well groomed and looking fine, to the leading cart. If you ask how he harnessed him, well, he did it in this way. First, he fastened the yoke on to the pole. Then he put the bull in on one side and fastened a smooth piece of wood from the cross yoke on to the axle so that the yoke was tight and could not bend. Thus a single bull could pull a cart that was designed to be pulled by two oxen.

28: Nandivisāla Jātaka,
The Bull Who Won the Bet

So now seated on the pole, the brahmin stroked Nandi Visāla on the back and called on him in this style, "Now then, my fine fellow! Pull them along, my fine fellow!" With a single pull the Bodhisatta tugged along the whole string of one hundred carts until the last cart stood where the first cart had started. The merchant, rich in herds, paid up the two thousand gold pieces. Other people, too, gave large sums to the Bodhisatta and all of it went to the brahmin. Thus he gained greatly because of the Bodhisatta.

Figure: The Mighty Bull Pulls One Hundred Carts!

In this way he rebuked the Six by showing that harsh words please no one. The Master, as Buddha, uttered this stanza:

Speak only words of kindness, never words
Unkind. For he who spoke kindly, he moved
A heavy load, and brought him wealth, for love.

When he ended his lesson about speaking only words of kindness, the Master identified the birth by saying, "Ānanda was the brahmin of those days, and I myself Nandi Visāla."

29: Kaṇha Jātaka,
The Old Woman's Black Bull

This story references the "double miracle," also called the "twin miracle":

"In Sravasti, standing on a jeweled walk, the Buddha proceeded to perform the Yamaka-pātihāriya (Twin Miracle), unattainable to any disciple and so called because it consisted in the appearance of phenomena of opposite character in pairs, e.g. emitting flames from the upper part of his body and a stream of water from the lower, and then alternatively. Flames of fire and streams of water also proceeded alternatively from the right side of his body and from the left." – [Wikipedia]

The Buddha performed these miracles after six teachers of opposing Dharmas claimed to be able to perform miracles but they were unable to do so.

The real importance of the miracles, however, was that because of this incident the Buddha made a monastic rule that forbid his disciples from displaying any supernormal powers. This is why people like the Dalai Lama, who is supposed to be able to levitate, never reveal their abilities. Even mind reading, which is probably the most common supernormal power, cannot be displayed without breaking the monastic code.

"With heavy loads." This story was told by the Master while at Jetavana, about the Double Miracle, which, together with the Descent from Heaven, will be related in the Thirteenth Book, in the Sarabhamiga Jātaka (*Jātaka 483*).

After he performed the Double Miracle and spent some time in heaven, the all-knowing Buddha descended into the city of Saṁkassa on the day of the Great Pavāraṇā Festival (*this happens just after the annual rains retreat*) and then went to Jetavana with a large following.

Gathering together in the Dharma Hall, the monks sat praising the virtues of the Master, saying, "Sirs, the Buddha is without peer. No one can surpass the Buddha. The Six teachers, though they often said that they, and they only, could perform miracles, were not able to produce a single one. Oh! How peerless is the Master!"

The Buddha entered the Dharma Hall and asked them what they were discussing. They told the Master that they were talking about his own

29: Kaṇha Jātaka,
The Old Woman's Black Bull

virtues. "Monks," the Master said, "who shall bear the yoke borne by me? Even in bygone days, when I came to life as an animal, I was unsurpassed." And, so saying, he told this story of the past.

Once upon a time when Brahmadatta was reigning in Benares, the Bodhisatta was born as a bull. When he was still a young calf, his owners, who had been living with an old woman, gave him to her as payment for their lodging. She raised him like her own child, feeding him on rice pudding and fine rice and on other good food. He became known as "Granny's Blackie." As he was growing up, he used to roam about with the other cattle of the village, and he was as black as coal. The village children used to catch hold of his horns and ears and dewlaps (*a fold of loose skin hanging from the neck*) and go for a ride, or they would hold on to his tail and ride on his back.

One day he thought to himself, "My mother is very poor. She has painstakingly raised me as if I were her own child. What if I were to earn some money to ease her hardship?" After that he was always looking out for a way to earn some money.

One day a young merchant at the head of a caravan came with 500 wagons to a ford in the river. But the ford was so rough that his oxen could not pull the wagons across. Even when he took out all 500 pairs of oxen and yoked them together to form one team, they could not get a single cart across the river.

Close by that ford the Bodhisatta was with the other cattle of the village. The young merchant, being a judge of cattle, looked over the herd to see if there was a thoroughbred bull who could pull the wagons across. When he saw the Bodhisatta, he felt sure he would do. To find out who owned the Bodhisatta he said to the herdsmen, "Who owns this animal? If I could use him to get my wagons across, I would pay for his services." They said, "Take him and harness him, then, for he does not have a master."

But when the young merchant slipped a rope through the Bodhisatta's nose and tried to lead him off, the bull would not budge. For, we are told, the Bodhisatta would not go until his fee was arranged. Understanding his meaning, the merchant said, "Master, if you will pull these 500 wagons across, I will pay you two coins per cart, or a thousand coins in all."

The Bodhisatta then proceeded to help. Away he went, and the men harnessed him to the carts. He dragged the first cart with a single pull and landed it high and dry. And he continued until he had hauled over the whole string of wagons.

The young merchant tied a bundle containing 500 coins around the Bodhisatta's neck, or at the rate of only one coin for each cart. The Bodhisatta thought to himself, "This fellow is not paying what we agreed! I won't let him move on!" So he stood across the path of the first wagon and blocked the way. And as much as they tried, they could not get him out of the way. "I suppose he knows that I did not pay him properly," the merchant thought. So he put 1,000 coins in a bundle and tied it around the Bodhisatta's neck, saying, "Here's your pay for pulling the wagons across." And away went the Bodhisatta with the 1,000 coins to his "mother."

Figure: Don't Try to Cheat This Bull!

"What's that around Blackie's neck?" cried the children of the village, running up to him. But the Bodhisatta charged at them and made them run off so that he could reach his "mother" all right. When he got there, he was very tired. His eyes were bloodshot from dragging the 500 wagons over the river. The pious woman, finding 1,000 coins around

29: Kaṇha Jātaka,
The Old Woman's Black Bull

his neck, cried out, "Where did you get this, my child?" The herdsmen told her what had happened, and she exclaimed, "Have I ever said that I want to make money from you, my child? Why did you go through all this effort?" She washed the Bodhisatta with warm water and rubbed him all over with oil. She gave him water to drink and fed him fine food. And when her life ended, she passed away, with the Bodhisatta, to fare according to her karma.

When he ended this lesson to show that the Buddha was unmatched in the past as then, he showed the connection by uttering this stanza:

> *With heavy loads to carry, with bad roads,*
> *They harness "Blackie." He soon pulls the load.*

After his lesson to show that only "Blackie" could pull the wagons, he showed the connection and identified the birth by saying, "Uppalavaṇṇā was the old woman of those days, and I myself 'Granny's Blackie.'" (*Uppalavaṇṇā was one of the two chief nuns. The other was Khema.*)

30: Muṇika Jātaka,
The Ox Who Envied the Pig

This story might also be called, "Be careful what you wish for!"

You may notice that the Buddha's attendant, Ānanda, shows up in many of these stories, and not always in the most flattering way. There was a lot of jealousy of Ānanda in the Sangha because he was so close to the Buddha, and he controlled access to the Buddha. Ānanda was also, according to the Pāli texts, most responsible for getting the Buddha to ordain women. This was very unpopular among the monks. So in the Jātaka literature, presumably this is why he shows up so often as the story's foil.

"Do not envy poor Muṇika." This story was told by the Master while at Jetavana. It is about a monk who was being seduced by a plump young woman, as will be related in the Thirteenth Book in the Culla Nārada Kassapa Jātaka (*Jātaka 477*).

The Master asked the monk, "Is it true, brother, as they say, that you are being tempted by a young woman?"

"It is true, sir," he replied.

"Brother," the Master said, "she is your ruination. Even in bygone days, you met your end and were made into a feast for the guests on her wedding day." And so saying, he told this story of the past.

Once upon a time, when Brahmadatta was reigning in Benares, the Bodhisatta was born as an ox named Big Red. He lived on a wealthy man's estate in a certain town. He had a younger brother who was known as Little Red. They were the only two oxen on the estate to do all the work for the family.

The wealthy man had an only daughter. A gentleman of the town asked for her hand in marriage for his son. The wealthy man and his wife agreed to the match. And they wanted to provide the finest food for the wedding guests, so they began to fatten up a pig named Muṇika.

When Little Red saw this he said to his brother, "You and I have to do all of the heavy work for this household, but all they give us for our

30: Muṇika Jātaka,
The Ox Who Envied the Pig

pains is sorry grass and straw to eat. Yet here is the pig being fed on fine rice! Why does he deserve to get such good food?"

His brother said, "My dear Little Red, do not be jealous of him, for the pig eats the food of death. He is being fattened to provide a feast for the guests at their daughter's wedding. The guests will be coming any day now. Then you will see that pig pulled out of his pen by the legs, killed, and converted into curry!" And so saying, he repeated this verse:

> *Do not envy poor Muṇika. It is death*
> *He eats. Be contented with your frugal fare.*
> *It is the guarantee of many days to come.*

Figure: Beware of farmers bearing gifts!

Soon afterwards the guests did arrive, and Muṇika was killed and cooked into all manner of dishes. The Bodhisatta said to Little Red, "Did you see Muṇika, dear brother?"

"I did indeed, brother, see the outcome of Muṇika's feasting. It is better to have a hundred, even a thousand, times worse food than we have, even if it is just grass, straw, and trash. For our food does not lead to harm, and it guarantees that our lives will not be cut short!"

When he ended his lesson about how the monk had been brought to his doom by that young woman and had been made into a feast for the wedding guests, he taught the Four Noble Truths. After he finished, the tempted monk attained the first stage of awakening, stream-entry. The Master then showed the connection and identified the birth by saying, "The tempted monk was the pig Muṇika of those days. The young woman is the same in both cases. Ānanda was Little Red, and I myself Big Red."

31: Kulāvaka Jātaka,
On Mercy to Animals

This story in the present has as a water strainer as its central object. Monks and nuns at the time of the Buddha were only allowed eight possessions: 1) an outer robe, 2) an inner robe, 3) a thick robe for the winter, 4) an alms bowl for food, 5) a razor for shaving, 6) a needle and thread, 7) a belt, and 8) a water strainer. The water strainer was for removing impurities from the water, but as noted here, it was also to strain out tiny, living creatures so that the monks and nuns would not inadvertently kill them.

This feels to me like somewhat more of a Jain theme than a Buddhist one. The Jain religion is very strict about non-harming. They even wear masks across their faces so they do not accidentally inhale and kill tiny bugs. However it came to be, it is still a lovely example of being considerate and compassionate to all living beings, no matter how tiny they are.

The Jātaka Tale itself is quite long and rambling. It can be divided into four parts. In the first part the Bodhisatta convinces the men of the village to devote their lives to doing good deeds and following the Five Moral Precepts (Not killing, not stealing, refraining from sexual misconduct, not lying, and not using intoxicants.). However, this makes the head of the village angry because he used to make money from their drinking and bad behavior. So he goes to the King and accuses them of being criminals. However, because of their virtue they are able to gain the King's favor and are given control of the village.

In the second part of the story the Bodhisatta and his men build a great hall at the main intersection in the town. However, they exclude women from their good works. But a woman named "Goodness" conspires with the carpenter to build a pinnacle for the building. After this, two other women also contribute to the building project, and the village grows and prospers.

In the third part, the Bodhisatta is reborn as Sakka, the King of the Devas. He fights a war against the Asuras, who are demi-gods. In this part of the story, Sakka is fighting the Asuras using his powerful chariot. But because his action is accidentally killing Garuḷas (these are creatures that are half man and half bird) he stops, even though it means he may lose the battle.

In the fourth part of the story we follow the fates of four women, three of whom are the ones who contributed to the village building project. They are reborn in a high heavenly realm because of their generosity. However, a fourth woman has a low rebirth as a crane because she did not do any acts of merit during her life. Sakka finds her and teaches her to keep the Five Precepts, and because of her ensuing virtue ends up as the wife of Sakka.

The idea of merit may sound rather mercenary to a Western audience, but it is a very important theme in Buddhism. One gains merit by good and wholesome acts. They have as their fruit a good rebirth. And of course, the purer and more sincere the act is, the greater the merit. Everybody wins.

"Save all the forest's children." This story was told by the Master while at Jetavana. It is about a monk who drank water without straining it.

Tradition says that two young monks who were friends went from Sāvatthi into the country to live in a pleasant spot. After staying there as long as they wanted, they left and set out for Jetavana in order to see the Perfect Buddha.

One of them carried a strainer, but the other one did not have one so both of them used the same strainer before drinking. One day they had an argument. As a result, the owner of the strainer did not let his companion use it, and he strained and drank alone by himself.

Because the other monk was not allowed to use the strainer, he drank water without straining it. Eventually they both reached Jetavana, and after saluting the Master, they took their seats. After greeting the two monks, he asked where they came from.

"Sir," they said, "we have been living in a town in the Kosala country. We came here to see you."

"I trust you have arrived as good friends, just as you did when you started?" the Buddha said.

The brother without a strainer said, "Sir, we had an argument on the road, and he would not lend me his strainer."

The other monk said, "Sir, he didn't strain his water, but intentionally drank it down with all the living things it contained."

"Is this true, brother, that you intentionally drank water with all the living things it contained?"

"Yes, sir, I did drink unstrained water," he replied.

"Brother, in bygone days there were wise and good men who were fleeing an enemy after they had been routed. This was in the days of

31: Kulāvaka Jātaka,
On Mercy to Animals

their sovereignty over the City of the Devas. But they would not kill living creatures even to win the battle. Rather, they turned their chariots back, sacrificing great glory in order to save the lives of the children of the Garuḷas." And, so saying, he told this story of the past.

Once upon a time there was a king of Magadha reigning at Rājagaha. The Bodhisatta was born in those days as a young noble. He was named "Prince Magha," but when he grew up, he became known as "Magha the young Brahmin." His parents arranged a marriage for him with a young woman from a family of equal rank. And he, with a family of sons and daughters growing up around him, was very generous and charitable, and he kept the Five Precepts.

There were just thirty families in the village, and one day the men were standing in the middle of the village conducting their affairs. The Bodhisatta cleared aside the dust from where he was standing and was standing there in comfort, when another man came and took his place there. Then the Bodhisatta made himself another comfortable standing place, only to have it taken from him like the first. Again and again the Bodhisatta cleared a space until he had made comfortable standing places for every man there.

On another occasion he put up a pavilion. Later on he pulled it down and built a hall with benches and a jar of water inside. Over time these thirty men were led by the Bodhisatta to become like him. He established them in the Five Precepts, after which they used to go around with him doing good works. They were always in the Bodhisatta's company. They used to get up early and go out with razors and axes and clubs in their hands. They used to roll all of the stones out of the way that lay on the four highways and other roads of the village. They cut down any trees that would scrape against the axles of chariots. They smoothed out rough places on the roads. They built causeways, dug water tanks, and built a hall. They showed charity and kept the Precepts. In this way the villagers followed the Bodhisatta's teachings.

The head of the village, however, thought to himself, "When these men used to get drunk and commit crimes, I would make a lot of money by selling them drinks and by the fines they paid. But now here is this young brahmin Magha who is making them keep the Precepts.

He is putting a stop to murders and other crime." And in his rage he cried, "I'll make them keep the Five Precepts!"

So he went to the King and said, "Sire, there is a band of robbers going about sacking villages and committing other crimes." When the King heard this, he sent his headman to go and bring the men back to him. They were brought back and presented as prisoners to the King. Without giving them a chance to defend themselves, the King proclaimed that they should be trampled to death by an elephant. They were forced to lie down in the King's courtyard, and the King sent for the elephant. The Bodhisatta encouraged the men, saying, "Remember the Precepts. Love the slanderer, the King, and the elephant as yourselves." And so they did.

Then the elephant was brought in to trample them to death. Yet no matter what they did, the elephant would not go near them. Instead he ran away trumpeting loudly. Elephant after elephant was brought up, but they all ran away like the first elephant. Thinking that the men must be using some drug on the elephants, the King ordered them to be searched. They did the search but found nothing, and they reported this to the King. "Then they must be using a spell," said the King. "Ask them whether they are using a spell."

The question was put to them, and the Bodhisatta said they, indeed, had a spell. The King's people told this to his majesty. So the King summoned them to him, and he said, "Tell me your spell."

The Bodhisatta replied, "Sire, this is our spell. No one among the whole thirty of us destroys life. We do not take what is not freely given. We do not commit any acts of wrongdoing, and we do not lie. We do not use intoxicants to the point of heedlessness. We abound in lovingkindness. We show charity. We level the roads, dig tanks, and we built a public hall. This is our spell, our safeguard, and our strength."

The King was very pleased with this, and he gave them everything the slanderer owned and made him their slave. He even gave them the elephant and the village.

* * *

After this they were able to do good works to their hearts' content. They sent for a carpenter and had him build a large hall at the junction of the four highways. But because they had lost all desire for women, they would not let any woman share in the good work.

31: Kulāvaka Jātaka,
On Mercy to Animals

Now in those days there were four women in the Bodhisatta's house. Their names were Goodness, Thoughtful, Joy, and Highborn. Goodness, finding herself alone with the carpenter, bribed him, saying, "Brother, please help make me the main benefactor of this hall."

"Very well," he said. And before doing any other work on the building, he had some of his finest wood dried. He made it into a pinnacle for the building. He wrapped it up in cloth and laid it aside. When the hall was finished and it was time to put on the pinnacle, he exclaimed, "Alas, my masters, there's one thing we have not made."

"What is that?"

"Why, we ought to have a pinnacle."

"All right, let's get one."

"But it can't be made out of green wood. We need a pinnacle made from wood that was cut some time ago, and then fashioned and bored and set aside."

"Well, what can we do now?"

"Why, let me look around and see if anybody has a pinnacle on his house that might be for sale." As they looked around, they found one in the house of Goodness. But she would not sell it to them. "If you will make me a partner in the good work," she said, "I will give it you for nothing."

"No," they replied, "we do not let women share in our good work."

Then the carpenter said to them, "My masters, why do you say this? There is no place from which women are excluded. Take the pinnacle, and our work will be complete."

So they agreed. They took the pinnacle and completed their hall. They had benches installed. They put jars of water inside and provided a constant supply of boiled rice. They built a wall around the hall with a gate. They put sand inside the wall and planted a row of palm trees. The lady Thoughtful planted a pleasure garden there, and she planted every variety of flowering or fruit-bearing tree. Joy had a water tank dug there, and she covered it with the five kinds of lotuses. It was beautiful to behold. However, the lady Highborn did nothing.

The Bodhisatta fulfilled these seven mandates: to cherish one's mother, to cherish one's father, to honor one's elders, to speak the truth, to avoid harsh speech, to avoid slander, and to be generous.

Whoever supports his parents, honors age,
Is gentle, friendly, does not slander,
Is generous, truthful, and is not harsh,
Even the Thirty-Three shall hail him as Good.

(*The Thirty-Three is one of the heavenly realms in the Buddhist cosmology. It is called that because it is ruled by 33 devas, or gods.*)

The town grew to be highly renowned, and when he died the Bodhisatta was reborn in the Realm of the Thirty-Three as Sakka, King of Devas. His friends were also reborn there.

* * *

In those days there were Asuras (*demigods*) living in the Realm of the Thirty-Three. Sakka, King of Devas, said "What good is a kingdom for us that we have to share? So he got the Asuras drunk and threw them by their feet onto the slopes of Mount Sineru. (*Mount Sineru is the sacred five-peaked mountain that is the center of the spiritual universe.*) They tumbled back down to "The Asura Realm," as it is called. This is a region on the lowest level of Mount Sineru. It is equal in size to the Realm of the Thirty-Three. There is a tree there that resembles the Coral Tree of the Devas that lasts for an aeon. It is called the Pied Trumpet-flower. (*The Coral Tree of the Devas lasts one kalpa, as stated here. A kalpa is a life of the universe, i.e., the big bang, followed by expansion and then contraction of the universe.*) However, they could tell by the blossoms of this tree that this was not the Realm of Devas where the Coral Tree blooms. So they cried, "Old Sakka got us drunk and threw us into the great deep, throwing us out of our heavenly city."

"Come," they shouted. "Let us win back our realm from him by force of arms." And they climbed up the sides of Sineru like ants up a pillar.

Hearing that the Asuras were coming, Sakka went out into the great deep to fight them, but he was driven back. He turned and ran away along crest after crest of the southern deep in his "Chariot of Victory," which was over 500 miles long.

Now as his chariot sped along the deep, it came to the Forest of the Silk-Cotton Trees. As the chariot flew by, these mighty trees were

31: Kulāvaka Jātaka,
On Mercy to Animals

mowed down like so many palms, and they fell into the deep. And as the children of the Garuḷas were in the deep, you could hear their cries. Sakka said to Mātali, his charioteer, "Mātali, my friend, what is that noise? It sounds heartrending."

"Sire, it is the cry of Garuḷas' children in their fear. Their forest is being destroyed by the rush of your chariot."

Sakka said, "Do not let them be afraid because of me, friend Mātali. Let us not, for the sake of conquest, destroy life. Rather I will, for their sake, give my life as a sacrifice to the Asuras. Turn the chariot back."

And so saying, he repeated this stanza:

> Let the forest's children, Mātali,
> Escape our all-devouring chariot.
> I offer up, a willing sacrifice,
> My life to the Asuras. These poor birds
> Shall not, through me, be torn from their nests.

Figure: Sakka Hears the Cries of the Garuḷas' Children

Mātali, the charioteer, turned the chariot around and went to the Realm of Devas by a different route. But the moment the Asuras saw him turn his chariot round, they cried out that the Sakkas of other worlds must surely be coming up. "It must be his reinforcements that make him turn his chariot around." Trembling for their lives, they all ran away and never stopped until they were back in the Asura Realm. And Sakka, entering heaven, stood in the midst of his city surrounded by his devas and of Brahma's angels. And at that moment through a tear in the earth a Victory Palace 3,500 miles high arose. Then, to prevent the Asuras from coming back again, Sakka sent guards in five places, about which it was said:

> Both cities are impregnable!
> The five guards watch Nāgas, Garuḷas,
> Gandhabba, Kumbaṇḍhas, and the Four Great Kings!

(*The Nāgas are half man, half serpent. The Gandhabbas are beings in the lowest heavenly realm. Kumbaṇḍhas are goblins. All three of these types of beings live in the Realm of the Four Heavenly Kings, which is just above the human realm. In the Buddhist cosmology, it is the lowest of the heavenly realms.*)

* * *

But when Sakka was enjoying the glory of heaven as the King of Devas, safely protected by the guards at these five posts, Goodness died and was reborn as his handmaiden. Because of her gift of the pinnacle, a mansion sprang up for her. It was named "Goodness." It was studded with heavenly jewels 1,500 miles high. Sakka sat under the white heavenly canopy of royal state, the King of Devas, ruling men and Devas.

The lady Thoughtful, too, died. She was also reborn as a handmaiden of Sakka. The effect of her building the pleasure garden was that there arose a pleasure garden called "Thoughtful's Vine Grove." The lady Joy, too, died, and she was likewise reborn as one of Sakka's handmaidens. The fruit of her water tank was that there arose a tank called "Joy" that was named after her. But Highborn, who had not performed any acts of merit, was reborn as a crane in a cave in the forest.

"There's no sign of Highborn," Sakka said to himself. "I wonder where she was reborn." And as he was thinking about it, he found her. So he paid her a visit and brought her back with him to heaven. He showed her the delightful city of the Devas, the Hall of Goodness,

31: Kulāvaka Jātaka,
On Mercy to Animals

Thoughtful's Vine Grove, and the tank called Joy. "These three," Sakka said, "have been reborn as my handmaidens because of the good works they did. But you, having done no good work, were reborn in bad circumstances. From now on you should keep the Precepts." And having encouraged her in this way and established her in the Five Precepts, he took her back and let her go free. And from then on, she did keep the Precepts.

A short time afterwards, being curious as to whether she was able to keep the Precepts, Sakka went and lay down in front of her in the shape of a fish. Thinking the fish was dead, the crane seized it by the head. The fish wagged its tail. "Why, I do believe it's alive," the crane said, and she let the fish go. "Very good, very good," Sakka said. "You will be able to keep the Precepts." And so saying he went away.

When she died as a crane, Highborn was reborn into the family of a potter in Benares. Wondering where she had gone, he was able to find where she was. Sakka disguised himself as an old man. He filled a cart with cucumbers of solid gold and sat in the middle of the village. He cried out, "Buy my cucumbers! Buy my cucumbers!" People came to him and asked for them. "I only give them to people who keep the Precepts," he said. "Do you keep them?"

"We don't know what you mean by your 'Precepts.' Sell us the cucumbers."

"No. I don't want money for my cucumbers. I give them away but only to those who keep the Precepts."

"Who is this clown?" the people said as they turned away. Hearing this, Highborn thought to herself that the cucumbers must have been brought for her, and she went and asked for some. "Do you keep the Precepts, madam?" he said. "Yes, I do," she replied.

"I brought these here for you and you alone," he said, and he left the cucumbers, the cart, and everything at her door.

Highborn continued to keep the Precepts for her entire life. After she died she was reborn as the daughter of the Asura King Vepacittiya, and she was rewarded for her goodness with the gift of great beauty. When she grew up, her father gathered the Asuras together and give his daughter the choice of any of them for a husband. And Sakka, who had searched and found out where she was, took the shape of an

Asura. He came down and said to himself, "If Highborn chooses a husband truly after her own heart, I will be the one she chooses."

Highborn was dressed and brought to the place of assembly. There she was told to select a husband after her own heart. She looked around and saw Sakka. She was moved by her love for him in a past existence and chose him for her husband. Sakka carried her off to the city of the devas and made her the chief of 25 million dancing girls. And when his life ended, he passed away to fare according to his karma.

His lesson ended, the Master rebuked that monk with these words: "Thus, monks, the wise and good of bygone days when they were rulers of the Devas, even at the sacrifice of their own lives would not kill. And can you, who have taken an oath, drink unstrained water with all the living creatures in it?" And he showed the connection and identified the birth, by saying, "Ānanda was Mātali the charioteer, and I was Sakka."

32: Nacca Jātaka,
The Animals Choose Kings

The Buddhist texts are not shy about telling graphic stores. In this one, a misbehaving monk exposes himself defiantly to the Buddha. This just shows that life is life, even for a Buddha.

"*A pleasing note.*" This story was told by the Master while at Jetavana, about a monk who had many possessions. The incident is the same as in the Devadhamma Jātaka (*Jātaka 6*).

"Is this report true, Brother," the Master said, "that you have many possessions?"

"Yes, sir."

"Why do you have so many possessions?"

Without listening further, the monk tore off his clothes and stood stark naked before the Master, crying, "I'll go about like this!"

"My goodness!" everyone exclaimed. The man ran away and went back to his life as a layperson. Gathering together in the Dharma Hall, the monks talked of his impropriety in behaving that way in front of the Master. Just then the Master came in and asked what they were talking about. "Sir," they answered, "we were discussing the impropriety of that monk, and saying that in your presence and right before all the four classes of your followers (*monks, nuns, laymen, and laywomen*) he lost all sense of shame and stood there stark naked as a mischievous child. Then seeing that he was repudiated by everyone, he lost the faith and lapsed back into a low life."

The Master said, "Monks, this is not the only loss his shamelessness has caused him. In bygone days he lost a jewel of a wife just as he now has lost the jewel of the faith." And so saying, he told this story of the past.

Once upon a time, in the first cycle of the world's history, the four-legged animals chose the lion as their king, the fish chose the monster fish, and the birds chose the golden mallard.

Now the King Golden Mallard had a lovely young daughter, and her royal father granted her any favor that she might ask. The request she made was to be allowed to choose a husband for herself. The King in fulfillment of his promise gathered all the birds together in the country of the Himalayas. All kinds of birds came, swans and peacocks and all other birds. They flocked together on a great plateau of bare rock. Then the King sent for his daughter and told her to go and choose a husband after her own heart.

As she looked over the crowd of birds, her eye landed on the peacock with his neck of jeweled sheen and tail of different colors. She chose him, saying, "Let this be my husband." Then the assembly of the birds went up to the peacock and said, "Friend peacock, this princess has chosen you from among all these birds."

Carried away by his extreme joy, the peacock exclaimed, "Until today you have never seen how excited I am!" And in defiance of all decency he spread his wings and began to dance, and in dancing he exposed himself.

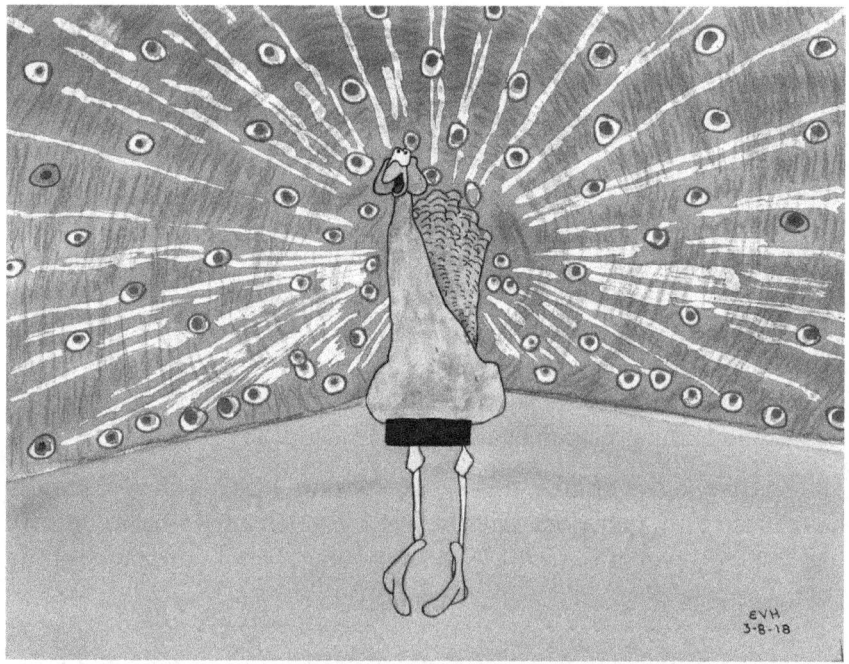

Figure: The Peacock's Embarrassing Dance

Filled with shame, King Golden Mallard said, "This fellow has neither modesty within his heart nor decency in his outward behavior. I certainly will not give my daughter to one who is so shameless." And there in the midst of all the birds, he repeated this stanza:

32: Nacca Jātaka,
The Animals Choose Kings

A pleasing note is yours, a lovely back,
A neck in hue like a precious stone.
Your outstretched feathers reach the height of a man.
But your dancing loses you, my child.

In front of the whole gathering King Royal Mallard gave his daughter to a young mallard, a nephew of his. Covered with shame at the loss of the mallard princess, the peacock rose straight up from the place and fled away. And King Golden Mallard too went back to his dwelling place.

"Thus, monks," the Master said, "this is not the only time his breach of modesty has caused him a loss. Just as it has now caused him to lose the jewel of the faith, so in bygone days it lost him a jewel of a wife." When he ended this lesson, he showed the connection and identified the birth by saying, "The monk with the many possessions was the peacock of those days, and I myself the Royal Mallard."

33: Sammodamāna Jātaka, *The Quarrel of the Quails*

There are a couple of interesting moments in this story. First, when the quail hunter sees what the birds are doing, he doesn't flinch. He assumes that sooner or later the harmony that enables the birds to outwit him will not last. He seems to have a pretty good idea about the nature of the quails in that community.

The second interesting moment is when the Bodhisatta sees the dispute, and he simply leaves. This is a common theme in the Buddha's teaching. The hardest thing to do when there is a problem is nothing, but that is often the best choice. The Bodhisatta has enough discernment to see that there is nothing to be done. This couples the qualities of discernment (wisdom) and equanimity. We often do harm by trying to intervene when it is inappropriate. The reason that we do this is the impulse to act. We need equanimity to calm these impulses, and we also need wisdom to see what actions are skillful and which ones are not.

"While harmony reigns." This story was told by the Master while living in the Banyan Grove near Kapilavatthu. It is about a squabble over a head scarf, as will be related in the Kuṇāla Jātaka (*Jātaka* 536).

On this occasion, however, the Master said this to some royal kinsfolk: "My lords, strife among kinsfolk is unseemly. Yes, in bygone times, animals, who had defeated their enemies when they lived in harmony, came to utter destruction when they argued." And at the request of his royal kinsfolk, he told this story of the past.

Once upon a time when Brahmadatta was King of Benares, the Bodhisatta was born as a quail, and he lived in the forest at the head of many thousands of quails. In those days there was a fowler who caught quails who came to that place. He used to imitate the song of a quail until he saw that the birds had gathered together. Then he would throw his net over them and lash the sides of the net together to trap them. Then he crammed them into a basket and went home to sell his prey for a living.

Now one day the Bodhisatta said to the quails, "This fowler is creating havoc among our kinsfolk. I know a way to make it impossible for him to catch us. When he throws the net over you, everyone should put his

33: Sammodamāna Jātaka,
The Quarrel of the Quails

head through the mesh, and then all of you must fly away together with the net and land on some thorn bushes. Once in the thorn bushes you can each escape from the net."

"Very good," they said, and they all nodded in agreement.

The next day, when the net was cast over them, they did just as the Bodhisatta had told them. They lifted up the net, flew off, and landed in some thorn bushes. Then they escaped from underneath the net. The fowler eventually found his net, and while he was still disentangling it, evening came on, and he went away empty-handed.

On the next day and following days the quails played the same trick. So it became the regular thing for the fowler to be engaged until sunset disentangling his net, and then to go home empty-handed. His wife grew angry and said, "Every day you come home empty-handed. I suppose you've got a second house somewhere to keep up!"

"No, my dear," the fowler said. "I do not have a second home to keep up. The fact is those quails have figured out how to work together. The moment my net is over them, they fly off with it and escape. Then they leave it in some thorn bushes. But I know that they won't continue to cooperate. Don't worry. As soon as they start arguing among themselves, I will bag the lot of them, and that will bring a smile to your face." And so saying, he repeated this stanza to his wife:

> While harmony reigns, the birds carry off the net.
> When quarrels arise, they'll fall prey to me.

Not long after this, one of the quails landed accidentally on another quail's head. "Who landed on my head?" this quail cried angrily. "I did, but I didn't mean to. Don't be angry," said the first quail. But despite this answer, the other quail remained angry. They began to taunt each other, saying, "I suppose it is you who single-handedly lifts up the net!" As they argued with one another, the Bodhisatta thought to himself, "There is no safety with one who is quarrelsome. The time has come when they will no longer lift up the net, and as a result they will come to destruction. The fowler will get his opportunity. I can stay here no longer." And with that he with his following went elsewhere.

Sure enough the fowler came back a few days later. He lured them by singing their song and then threw his net over them. Then one quail said, "They say that when you lifted the net all by yourself, the hair on your head came off. Now is your time. Lift away!" The other responded, "When you were lifting the net, they say both your wings molted. Now is *your* time. Lift away."

Figure: Oh, Those Quarreling Quail!

But while they were needling each other to lift the net, the fowler himself lifted the net for them. He crammed them into his basket and took them home. And his wife's face was wreathed with smiles.

"Thus, sires," the Master said, "quarreling among kinsfolk is unseemly. Quarrelling only leads to destruction." His lesson ended, he showed the connection and identified the birth by saying, "Devadatta was the foolish quail of those days, and I myself the wise and good quail."

34: Maccha Jātaka,
The Slave of Passion

There is an interesting point made in this story. The Bodhisatta is concerned about the state of mind of the fish if he dies at that moment. This is a common theme in the Buddhist tradition. Our next rebirth is determined by our past karma as well as the state of mind at the moment of death. This is why Buddhists hope for a very calm, loving, supportive environment when they die.

"*'Tis not the cold.*" This story was told by the Master while at Jetavana. It is about a monk who was seduced by his wife from his worldly life before joining the Saṅgha. The Master said on this occasion, "Is it true, as I hear, brother, that you have succumbed to passion?"

"Yes, Blessed One."

"Because of whom?"

"My former wife, sir, is sweet to touch. I cannot give her up!"

Then the Master said, "Brother, this woman is harmful to you. It was because of her that in bygone times you were about to meet your end when you were saved by me." And so saying, he told this story of the past.

Once upon a time when Brahmadatta was reigning in Benares, the Bodhisatta became his family's priest.

In those days some fishermen cast their net into the river. And a great big fish came along amorously toying with his wife. She, sensing the net as she swam ahead of him, circled around it and escaped. But her amorous spouse, blinded by passion, sailed right into the meshes of the net. As soon as the fishermen felt him in their net, they hauled it in and took the fish out.

They did not kill him at once but threw him alive on the sands. "We'll cook him in the coals for our meal," they said. Accordingly, they started to build a fire and carve a spit to roast him on. The fish lamented, saying to himself, "It's not the torture of the fire or the anguish of the spit or any other pain that hurts me. It is the distressing thought that my wife will be unhappy in the belief that I have gone off with someone else." And he repeated this stanza:

It's not the cold, the heat, or wounding net.
It's the fear my darling wife should think
Another's love has lured her spouse away.

Just then the priest came to the riverside with his attendants to bathe. Now he understood the language of all animals. Therefore, when he heard the fish's lament, he thought to himself, "This fish is suffering from passion. If he dies in this unhealthy state of mind, he cannot escape rebirth in hell. I will save him." So he went to the fishermen and said, "My men, don't you supply us with a fish every day for our curry?"

"What do you say, sir?" the fishermen said. "Take away any fish you want."

"We don't need any but this one. Only give us this one."

"He's yours, sir."

Figure: The Bodhisatta and the Love Lost Fish

Taking the fish in his two hands, the Bodhisatta sat down on the bank and said, "Friend fish, if I had not seen you today, you would have met your death. In the future stop being a slave of passion." And with

34: Maccha Jātaka,
The Slave of Passion

this exhortation he threw the fish into the water and went back into the city.

His lesson ended, the Master preached the Four Noble Truths, at the end of which the passionate monk won the First Path (*stream-entry*). Also, the Master showed the connection and identified the birth by saying, "The former wife was the female fish of those days, the passionate monk was the male fish, and I myself the family priest."

35: Vaṭṭaka Jātaka,
The Act of Truth

Miracles are a common theme in the Buddhist texts. This is a story about one of them.

Note again the reference to an "æon" or "kalpa," a life of the universe.

This story does not provide a very good example of parenting skills.

"*With wings that do not fly.*" The Master told this story while on an alms pilgrimage in Magadha. It is about the suppression of a forest fire.

Once the Master went on his morning alms round through a certain town in that country. On his return, after his meal, he went out again followed by a group of monks. Just then a great fire broke out. There were many monks both in front of the Master and behind him. The fire came on, spreading far and wide, until there was one sheet of smoke and flame.

Some unconverted samaṇa (*spiritual seekers who were not followers of the Buddha*) were overcome with fear. "Let us create a fire line," they cried, "and then the big fire will not sweep over the ground we have burned." And with this plan, they set about building a fire with their tinder sticks.

But others said, "What are you doing, brothers? It is as if you are blind to the moon in mid-heaven (*an astrological reference meaning someone who is very powerful*) or the sun rising brightly from the east or the sea on whose shores you stand or Mount Sineru towering before your very eyes. You are traveling with him who is peerless among devas and men alike. You do not give a thought to the All-Enlightened Buddha, but cry out, 'Let us create a fire line!' You do not know the might of a Buddha! Come, let us go to the Master."

Then, gathering all the samaṇa together, they flocked around the Lord of Wisdom. At a certain spot the Master halted, with this mighty assembly of samaṇa surrounding him. On rolled the flames, roaring as though to devour them. But when they approached the spot where the Buddha stood, the fire went out like a torch plunged into water. The fire was unable to spread into a space thirty-two lengths in diameter.

35: Vaṭṭaka Jātaka,
The Act of Truth

The samaṇa burst into praises of the Master, saying, "Oh! How great the virtues of a Buddha are! For even this fire, though lacking consciousness, could not sweep over the spot where a Buddha stood, but went out like a torch in water. Oh! How marvelous the powers of a Buddha are!"

Hearing their words, the Master said, "It is not my power in the present, brothers, that made this fire go out on reaching this spot of ground. It is the power of a former 'Act of Truth' of mine. For in this spot no fire will burn throughout the whole of this æon, the miracle being one that endures for an æon."

Then the Elder Ānanda folded a robe into four and spread it for the Master to sit on. The Master took his seat. Bowing to the Buddha as he sat cross-legged there, the brothers too seated themselves around him. Then they asked him, saying, "We only know about the present, sir. The past is hidden from us. Tell us about it." And, at their request, he told this story of the past.

Once upon a time in this spot in Magadha, the Bodhisatta was born as a quail. When he broke out of his shell, he became a young quail, about as big as a large ball. His parents kept him lying in the nest, while they fed him with food that they brought in their beaks. He did not have the strength to either spread his wings and fly through the air or to lift his feet and walk on the ground.

That spot was ravaged every year by a forest fire, and it was just at this time that the fire swept down on it with a mighty roaring. The flocks of birds, darting from their nests, were seized with the fear of death and flew shrieking away. The father and mother of the Bodhisatta were as frightened as the others, and they also flew away, leaving the Bodhisatta behind. Lying there in the nest, the Bodhisatta stretched out his neck, and seeing the flames spreading towards him, he thought to himself, "If I had the power to fly, I could get to safety. Or, if I could move my legs and walk, I could get there on foot. But my parents, seized with the fear of death, fled away to save themselves, leaving me here alone in the world. I am without protector or helper. What, then, shall I do?"

Then he had this thought: "There is in this world the Power of Goodness and the Power of Truth. There are those who, through

Jātaka Tales

having realized the Perfections in past ages, have become All-Enlightened beneath the Bodhi tree. They won Release by goodness, tranquility, and wisdom. They possess wisdom of the knowledge of Release. They are filled with truth, compassion, mercy, and patience, and their love embraces all creatures alike. Men call them transcendent Buddhas. There is a power that they won."

"I, too, grasp one truth. I hold and believe in a supreme goal. Therefore, I will call to mind the Buddhas of the past and the power they won. I will hold to the true belief in the supreme goal, and by the Power of Truth I will make the flames go back and save myself and the rest of the birds."

Then he said:

> There is saving grace in Goodness in this world.
> There is truth, compassion, and the purity of life.
> I will work a matchless miracle using the Power of Truth.
>
> Remembering Faith's might, and remembering
> those who triumphed in the days gone by,
> Strong in the truth, I will perform an Act of Truth.

Accordingly, the Bodhisatta, calling to mind the power of the Buddhas long since passed away, performed an Act of Truth in the name of the true faith that was in him, repeating this stanza:

> With wings that do not fly, feet that do not walk,
> Forsaken by my parents, here I lie!
> Wherefore I call upon you, dread Lord of Fire,
> Primeval Jātaveda, turn! Go back!

(*Jātaveda is the god of fire.*)

Even as he performed his Act of Truth, Jātaveda retreated to a space of sixteen lengths, and in going back the flames did not continue to devour everything in their path. They went out there and then, like a torch plunged in water. Therefore, it was said:

> I performed my Act of Truth, and with that
> The sheet of blazing fire left sixteen lengths
> Unscathed, like flames met by water and quenched.

And as that spot escaped being wasted by fire throughout a whole æon, the miracle is called an "æon miracle." When his life ended, the

35: Vaṭṭaka Jātaka,
The Act of Truth

Bodhisatta, who had performed this Act of Truth, passed away to fare according to his karma.

Figure: The Baby Quail Turns Back the God of Fire

(*Indian Gods are often androgynous.*)

"Thus, brothers," the Master said, "it is not my present power but the power of an Act of Truth performed by me when a young quail that made the flames pass over this spot in the forest." His lesson ended, he preached the Four Noble Truths, at the close of which some won the First (*stream-entry*), some the Second (*once-returner*), some the Third Path (*non-returner*), while others became Arahats. Also, the Master showed the connection and identified the birth by saying, "My present parents were the parents of those days, and I myself the king of the quails."

36: Sakuṇa Jātaka,
The Unsuitable Tree

This is a story about practicality. Many meditation teachers push and push and push, and this is not always the proper approach. You must learn to use good judgment. Just as weightlifters learned many years ago that you get stronger if you lift every other day rather than every day, meditators must learn to proceed in a skillful and wise manner. Of course, the path requires dedication, but if you push too hard you may actually regress.

"Citizens of the air." This story was told by the Master while at Jetavana. It is about a monk whose hut burned down.

Tradition says that a monk, having been given a theme for meditation by the Master, went from Jetavana to the land of Kosala. He lived there in a hut in a forest near a village. Now, during the very first month of his living there, his hut burned down. He told this to the villagers, saying, "My hut burned down. I live in discomfort." They responded, "The land is suffering from drought just now. We'll take care of when we have irrigated the fields."

When the irrigation was over, they said they must sow the seeds first. When they were done sowing the seeds, they had fences to build. When the fences were built, they had to do the weeding and the reaping and the threshing. With one job following after another, three months went by.

After three months spent in the open air in discomfort, that monk had developed his theme for meditation but he could get no further. So, after the Pavāraṇā festival which ends the Rainy Season, he went back again to the Master. With due salutation, he sat down next to him. After kindly words of greeting, the Master said, "Well, brother, have you lived happily through the Rainy Season? Did your theme for meditation end in success?" The monk told him what had happened, adding, "Because I did not have a suitable place to live, my theme did not end in success."

The Master said, "In bygone times, brother, even animals knew what suited them and what did not. How is it that you did not know?" And so saying, he told this story of the past.

Once upon a time when Brahmadatta was reigning in Benares, the Bodhisatta was born as a bird. He lived in a giant tree with branching

36: Sakuṇa Jātaka, The Unsuitable Tree

boughs at the head of a company of birds. Now one day, as the boughs of this tree were rubbing one against each other, dust began to fall. This was soon followed by smoke. When the Bodhisatta saw this, he thought to himself, "If these two boughs go on rubbing up against each other like this, they will catch fire. The fire will catch hold of the old leaves, and then the whole tree will catch fire as well. We cannot live here. The proper thing to do is to go somewhere else." And he repeated this stanza to the company of birds:

> *Citizens of the air, that in these boughs*
> *Have sought a place to live, see the seeds of fire*
> *This earthborn tree is breeding! Seek safety*
> *In flight! Our trusted stronghold harbors death!*

The wiser birds followed the Bodhisatta's advice and rose up in the air at once and went to live elsewhere. But the foolish ones said, "It is always like this with him. He is always seeing crocodiles in a drop of water." And so, not heeding the Bodhisatta's words, they stayed where they were. In a very short time, just as the Bodhisatta had predicted, flames broke out, and the tree caught fire. When the smoke and flame arose, the birds were blinded by the smoke, and they were unable to get away. One by one they dropped into the flames and were destroyed.

Figure: The Foolish Birds

"Thus, brothers," the Master said, "in bygone times even animals who were living in the treetop knew what suited them and what did not. How is it that you did not know?" His lesson ended, he preached the Four Noble Truths at the close of which that monk won the Fruit of the First Path (*stream-entry*). Then the Master showed the connection and identified the birth by saying, "The Buddha's disciples were the birds who listened to the Bodhisatta, and I myself was the wise and good bird."

37: Tittira Jātaka,
The Harmonious Friends

This is a story about respect for elders. This is not a popular theme in the West. It seems a little arbitrary, respecting someone just because they are older. But if you grow up in a culture that respects older people, it tends to work both ways. Young people respect their seniors, and seniors are expected to behave in a way that is worthy of respect. This point is made at the end of the story, where the partridge agrees to give wise advice in return for being given reverence.

A technical note is that in the Saṅgha, a nun or a monk's age is based on how many rains retreats they have had, not on their age. So a monk who is 60 years old but has only had one rains retreat is junior to someone who is 30 years old but has been to 10 of them.

This use of seniority comes from Sakyan Law. This is the law that the Buddha learned when he was growing up when his father was the raja of Sakya.

"They who honor age." This story was told by the Master while on his way to Sāvatthi. It is about how the Elder Sāriputta was kept out of a night's lodging.

When Anāthapiṇḍika finished building his monastery and sent word that it was complete, the Master left Rājagaha and went to Vesālī. He then set out again at his pleasure. The Six disciples (*the misbehaving monks we met in Jataka 28*) hurried on ahead, and before quarters could be set aside for the Elders, they took all of the available lodgings. They distributed these among their superiors, their teachers, and themselves. When the Elders came up later, there was no place for them to stay during the night. Even Sāriputta's disciples, for all their searching, could not find lodgings for the Elder. Being without shelter, Sāriputta spent the night at the foot of a tree near the Master's quarters, either walking up and down or sitting at the foot of the tree.

At early dawn the Master coughed as he came out. The Elder coughed too. "Who is that?" the Master asked.

"It is I, Sāriputta, sir."

"What are you doing here at this hour, Sāriputta?" Then the Elder told his story, at the close of which the Master thought, "Even now, while

I am still alive, the monks lack courtesy and respect. What will they not do when I am dead and gone?" That thought filled him with concern for the preservation of the Dharma.

As soon as day broke, he assembled the monks and asked them, "Is it true, brothers, that the followers of the Six went on ahead and kept the Elders among the Saṅgha out of lodgings for the night?"

"That is so, Blessed One," they replied.

With a reproof to the followers of the Six and as a lesson to all, he addressed the Saṅgha and said, "Tell me, who deserves the best lodging, the best water, and the best rice, brothers?"

Some answered, "Someone who was a nobleman before he became a monk." Others said, "Someone who was originally a brahmin, or a man of means." Others said, "The man versed in the Rules of the Order, the man who can expound the Law, or the men who have attained the first, second, third, or fourth jhāna." Others said, "The man who has attained the First, Second, or Third stage of awakening, or an Arahat, or one who knows the Three Great Truths (*that all conditioned things are impermanent, that this leads to suffering, and this makes conditioned existence imperfect and undesirable*), or one who has the Six Higher Knowledges (*also called the six supernormal powers: magical powers, the divine ear, reading the minds of others, knowledge of former existences, the divine eye, and the destruction of all defilements*)."

After the monks said who they thought was worthy of precedence in the matter of lodging and the like, the Master said, "In the Dharma that I teach, the standard by which precedence in the matter of lodging and the like is to be settled is not noble birth or having been a brahmin or having been wealthy before entering the Order. The standard is not familiarity with the Rules of the Order or with the Suttas. Nor is it the attainment of any of the four stages of jhāna or the attainment of any of the Four Stages of awakening. Brothers, in my religion it is seniority that claims respect of word and deed, salutation, and all due service. It is seniors who should enjoy the best lodging, the best water, and the best rice. This is the true standard, and therefore the senior monk ought to have these things. Yet, brothers, here is Sāriputta, who is my chief disciple, who has set the Wheel of the Dharma in motion, and who deserves to have a lodging next after myself. And Sāriputta spent

37: Tittira Jātaka,
The Harmonious Friends

the night without shelter at the foot of a tree! If you lack respect and deference even now, what will your behavior be as time goes by?"

And for their further instruction he said, "In times past, brothers, even animals came to the conclusion that it was not proper for them to live without respect and deference for one to another, or without the harmony of their common life. Even the animals decided to find out who among them was the most senior, and then to show him reverence. So they looked into the matter, and having found out which one of them was most senior, they showed him respect. And because of that they passed away at that life's end to be reborn in heaven." And so saying, he told this story of the past.

Once upon a time, near a great banyan tree on the slopes of the Himalayas, three friends lived together: a partridge, a monkey, and an elephant. But over time they lost respect and civility for one another, and they had no harmony in their lives. It occurred to them that it was not proper for them to live in this way. They decided that they should find out which one of them was the most senior, and that they should honor him.

As they were thinking about this, one day an idea struck them. As they sat together at the foot of that banyan tree, the partridge and the monkey said to the elephant, "Friend elephant, how big was this banyan when you first remember it?" The elephant said, "When I was a baby, this banyan was a mere bush. I used to walk over it, and as I stood next to it, its topmost branches used to just reach up to my belly. I've known the tree since it was a mere bush."

Next the monkey was asked the same question, and he replied, "My friends, when I was young, I could stretch out my neck as I sat on the ground, and I could eat the topmost sprouts of this banyan. So I've known this banyan since it was very tiny."

Then the partridge was asked the same question, and he said, "Friends, a long time ago there was a great banyan tree at this spot. I ate its seeds and excreted them here. That was the origin of this tree. Therefore, I have knowledge of this tree from before it was born, and I am older than both of you."

Then the monkey and the elephant said to the wise partridge, "Friend, you are the oldest. From now on you will be honored and venerated.

We will pay homage to you and respect your words and deeds. We will salute you, and we will follow your counsel. As for your part, from now on we ask that you give us your wise advice when we need it."

Figure: Paying Homage to the Elder

From then on, the partridge gave them wise counsel. He established them in the Five Precepts, which he also followed. Being established in the Precepts and being respectful and harmonious together, they lived together in peace. And when their lives came to an end, they were assured of rebirth in heaven.

"The aims of these three," the Master continued, "came to be known as the 'Holiness of the Partridge.' And if these three animals, brothers, could live together in respect and harmony, how can you, who have embraced the Rules of the Order that are so well-taught, live together without due respect and harmony? Therefore I proclaim, brothers, that you will respect the words and deeds of those who are most senior. You will salute them and be of service to them. They will be entitled to the best lodging, the best water, and the best rice. And never again will a senior be kept out of a lodging by a junior. If anyone keeps out his senior, then they commit an offense."

37: Tittira Jātaka,
The Harmonious Friends

At the close of this lesson the Master, as Buddha, repeated this stanza:

They who honor age are well versed in the Dharma.
Their reward is praise now and bliss hereafter.

When the Master finished speaking of the virtue of respecting age, he made the connection and identified the birth by saying, "Moggallāna was the elephant of those days, Sāriputta the monkey, and I myself the sage partridge."

38: Baka Jātaka,
The Crane and the Crab

This is a story about a cheater who gets cheated by an even more clever cheater. It might be called "What goes around comes around," which is our way of describing karma in the West.

"There is no benefit in deceit." The Master told this story while at Jetavana. It is about a monk who had been a tailor.

Tradition says that there was a monk at Jetavana who was exceedingly skillful in all operations to be performed with a robe, such as cutting, joining, arranging, and stitching. Because of his skill, he used to make robes and so he got the name of "The Robe Tailor." You might ask, what did he do? Well, he exercised his craft on old bits of cloth and turned out a nice soft robe. After the dyeing was done, he would make the old bits of cloth look like new by treating them with a wash containing flour to make a dressing. Then he would rub it with a shell until it looked quite smart and attractive. Then he would lay his handiwork aside.

Being ignorant of robe-making, the monks would come to him with brand-new cloth and say, "We don't know how to make robes. You make them for us."

"Sirs," he would reply, "a robe takes a long time to make. But I have one that I just finished. You can take it if you leave the new cloth in exchange." And, so saying, he would take the finished robe out and show it to them. And they, seeing its fine color and knowing nothing about what it was made of, thought it was a good strong robe. So they gave their brand new cloth to the "Robe Tailor" and went off with the robe he gave them. When it got dirty and it was washed in hot water, it revealed its true character, and the worn patches were visible here and there. Then the owners regretted their bargain. Eventually that monk became known for cheating all who came to him.

Now, there was a robe maker in a town who used to deceive everybody just as the brother did at Jetavana. This man's friends among the monks said to him, "Sir, they say that at Jetavana there is a robe maker who deceives everybody just like you." Then the thought struck him, "Come now, let me fool that city man!" So he made a very fine robe out of rags, and he dyed it a beautiful orange. He put this on

38: Baka Jātaka,
The Crane and the Crab

and went to Jetavana. The moment the other saw it, he coveted it and said to its owner, "Sir, did you make that robe?"

"Yes, I did, sir," was the reply.

"Let me have that robe, sir, and I will give you another one in its place."

"But, sir, we village monks find it hard to get the requisites. (*The requisites are food, medicine, clothing, and shelter.*) If I give this to you, what will I wear?"

"Sir, I have some brand-new cloth at my shelter. You can take it and make yourself a new robe."

"Reverend sir, I have shown you my own handiwork. But, if you want it, what can I do? Take it." And having deceived the other by exchanging the robe made from rags for the new cloth, he went on his way.

After wearing the botched robe, the Jetavana man washed it not long afterwards in warm water. He saw that it was made out of rags, and he was put to shame. The whole of the Saṅgha heard the news that the Jetavana man had been deceived by a tailor from the country.

Now, one day the monks were seated in the Dharma Hall discussing the news, when the Master entered and asked what they were talking about. They told him the story.

The Master said, "Monks, this is not the only instance of the Jetavana robe maker's deceitful tricks. In bygone times he did the same thing, and as he has been deceived now by someone from the country, so he was also in bygone times." And so saying, he told this story of the past.

Once upon a time the Bodhisatta was born in the forest as the fairy of a tree that stood near a certain lotus pond. In those days the water used to fall very low every summer in the pond. The pond was not very big, and there were many fish there. Catching sight of these fish, a certain crane said to himself, "I must find a way to trick and eat these fish." So he went and sat down in deep thought by the side of the water.

Now when the fish saw him, they said, "What are you thinking, my lord, as you sit there?"

"I am thinking about you," he replied.

"And what is your lordship thinking about us?"

"The water in this pool is very low, food is scarce, and the heat is intense. I was wondering to myself, as I sat here, how you fish will manage."

"And what are we to do, my lord?"

"Well, if you take my advice, I will pick you up one by one in my beak and carry you all off to a fine large pool covered with the five varieties of lotuses and put you down there."

"My lord," they said, "no crane ever cared about fish since the world began. You want to eat us one by one."

"No, I will not eat you if you trust me," the crane said. "If you don't believe me that there is such a pond, send one of you to go with me and see for himself." Believing the crane, they presented a great big fish to him (blind of one eye, by the way), who they thought would be a match for the crane, and they said, "Here's the one who will go with you."

The crane took off with the fish and put him in the pool, and after showing him the whole extent of it, brought him back again and put him in his old pond with the other fish. And he told them about the charms of the new pool.

After hearing this, they were eager to go there, and they said to the crane, "Very good, my lord. Please take us there."

The crane started with that big one-eyed fish. He carried him to the edge of the pool so that he could see the water, but he actually landed in a pear tree that grew on the bank. Throwing the fish down in a fork of the tree, he pecked it to death, and then he picked him clean and let the bones fall to the foot of the tree. Then back he went and said, "I've thrown him in. Who's next?" And so he took the fish one by one and ate them all until finally there were no fish left.

But there was still a crab remaining in the pond. So the crane, who wanted to eat him too, said, "Mister crab, I've taken all those fishes away and put them into a fine large pool covered all over with lotuses. Come along. I'll take you too."

"How will you carry me across?" the crab asked.

"Why, in my beak, to be sure," said the crane.

38: Baka Jātaka,
The Crane and the Crab

"Ah, but you might drop me like that," said the crab. "I won't go with you."

"Don't be frightened. I'll keep tight hold of you all the way."

The crab thought to himself, "He hasn't put the fish in the pool. If he does put me in, that would be great. But if he does not, why, I'll nip his head off and kill him." So he said to the crane, "You'd never be able to hold me tight enough, friend crane. But we crabs have got a very tight grip. If you let me take hold of your neck with my claws, I can hold tight and then I will go along with you."

Not suspecting that the crab wanted to trick him, the crane agreed. The crab gripped hold of the crane's neck with his claws like the pincers of a blacksmith, and he said, "Now you can start." The crane took him and showed him the pool first and then started off for the tree.

"The pool is this way, uncle," the crab said, "but you're taking me the other way."

"Very much your dear uncle I am!" said the crane, "and very much my nephew you are! I suppose you thought I am your slave to lift you up and carry you about! Just look at that heap of bones at the foot of the tree. I ate all those fish, so I will eat you too."

The crab said, "It was through their own folly that those fish were eaten by you. But I will not give you the chance to eat me. No. What I will do is to kill you. For you, fool that you were, did not see that I was tricking you. If we die, we will both die together. I'll chop your head clean off." And so saying he gripped the crane's throat with his claws like pincers. With his mouth wide open and tears streaming from his eyes, the crane, trembling for his life, said, "Lord, indeed I will not eat you! Spare my life!"

"Well, then, just fly to the pool and put me in," said the crab. Then the crane turned back and landed as directed to the pool and placed the crab on the mud at the water's edge. But the crab, before entering the water, nipped off the crane's head as deftly as if he were cutting a lotus stalk with a knife.

The tree fairy who lived in the tree saw this wonderful thing. He made the whole forest ring with applause and repeated this stanza in sweet tones:

Deceit does not profit the deceitful folk.
See what the deceitful crane got from the crab!

Figure: The Trickster Gets Tricked!

"Brothers," the Master said, "this is not the first time this fellow has been deceived by the robe maker from the country. In the past he was deceived in the same way." His lesson ended, he showed the connection and identified the birth, by saying, "The Jetavana robe maker was the crane of those days. The robe maker from the country was the crab, and I myself the tree fairy."

39: Nanda Jātaka,
Nanda and the Buried Gold

This story is about a person whose behavior changes dramatically if they are in a certain location. This may have to do with what in feng shui is called "location energy." We do not have that notion in the West, but it is common in Asian cultures.

Most people I know have been somewhere where they feel a very strong sense of energy. Two of which I am aware are Bodh Gaya, where the Buddha attained his awakening, and here in New Mexico at Chaco Canyon. These are positive location energy fields, but negative ones exist as well. You may have experienced this in a place where you felt a sudden sense of fear or dread. This may have to do with the location itself, or it may be due - at least in part - to your past karma and an experience related to that place.

"I think the gold..." This story was told by the Master while at Jetavana. It is about a student of Sāriputta.

Tradition says that this monk was obedient and dutiful and was devoted to caring for the Elder. Now, on one occasion the Elder took leave of the Master on an alms pilgrimage, and he went to South Magadha. When he got there, the monk suddenly grew so arrogant that he would not do what the Elder told him. Moreover, if he was asked, "Sir, do this," he argued with the Elder. The Elder could not understand what possessed him.

After making his pilgrimage, he went back again to Jetavana. The moment he got back to the monastery at Jetavana, the monk became the way he had always been.

The Elder told this to the Buddha, saying, "Sir, a student of mine in one place is like a slave bought for a hundred pieces, and in another he is so arrogant that a request to do anything makes him quarrelsome."

The Master said, "This is not the first time, Sāriputta, that he has shown this disposition. In the past too, if he went to one place, he was like a slave bought for a hundred pieces, while in another place, he became quarrelsome and contentious." And so, at the request of the Elder, he told this story of the past.

Once upon a time when Brahmadatta was reigning in Benares, the Bodhisatta was born as a nobleman. Another nobleman, a friend of his, was an old man. He had a young wife who had borne him a son and heir. The old man thought to himself, "As soon as I am dead, this girl, being as young as she is, will marry heaven knows who, and she will spend all my money instead of handing it over to my son. It would be my best course to hide my money and bury it safely in the ground."

So, in the company of a household slave of his named Nanda, he went to the forest and buried his riches at a certain spot. He said to the slave, "My good Nanda, show this treasure to my son after I am gone and don't let these woods be sold."

After giving this instruction to his slave, the old man died. In due course the son grew up and his mother said to him, "My son, your father, in the company of Nanda, buried his money. Get it back and look after the property of the family." So one day he said to Nanda, "Friend Nanda, did my father bury any treasure?"

"Yes, my lord."

"Where is it buried?"

"In the woods, my lord."

"Well, then, let us go there."

He took a shovel and a basket, and going to the scene, he said to Nanda, "Well, friend Nanda, where is the money?" But by the time Nanda got to the treasure and was standing right over it, he felt so self-important that he abused his master, saying, "You servant of a slave's son! Why should you have any money here?"

The young gentleman, pretending not to have heard this insolence, simply said, "Let us go then." He took the slave back home with him, and two or three days later, he returned to the place. But again Nanda abused him, as before. Without responding, the young gentleman went back and mulled the situation over in his mind. He thought to himself, "When we start out, this slave always means to tell me where the money is. But as soon as we get there, he starts abusing me. I do not understand the reason for this. I will talk to my father's old friend - the nobleman - about this." So he went to the Bodhisatta and told him what had happened. Then he asked his friend what the reason was for such behavior.

39: Nanda Jātaka, Nanda and the Buried Gold

Figure: Cranky Over Money

The Bodhisatta said, "The spot at which Nanda abuses you, my friend, is the place where your father's money is buried. Therefore, as soon as he starts abusing you again, say to him, 'Who are you talking to, you slave?' Pull him from his spot, take the spade, dig down, remove your family treasure, and make the slave carry it home for you." And so saying, he repeated this stanza:

> *I think the gold and jewels lie buried*
> *Where Nanda, low-born slave, so loudly wails!*

Taking respectful leave of the Bodhisatta, the young gentleman went home. He took Nanda to the spot where the money was buried.

Faithfully following the advice he had received, he took the money away and looked after the family property. He dutifully followed the Bodhisatta's counsel, and after a life spent in charity and other good works, he passed away to fare according to his karma.

Said the Master, "In the past this man had a similar disposition." His lesson ended, he showed the connection and identified the birth by saying, "Sāriputta's student was the Nanda of those days, and I the wise and good nobleman."

40: Khadiraṅgāra Jātaka, *The Pit of Coals*

This story is about the power of deep faith, resolve, and generosity.

There are several things worth knowing. First, according to the Buddhist tradition, the person that we know as the Buddha is one of many Buddhas throughout time. The idea is that a Buddha is born, awakens, and then teaches the Dharma. But eventually the teaching falls into decline and is lost. Eventually another Buddha is born, and the cycle begins again.

A Pacceka Buddha is a Buddha who awakens but decides not to teach the Dharma. Presumably this is because he does not think that anyone will understand it. This may be because of the era and the culture into which he is born.

Anāthapiṇḍika was the Buddha's foremost lay supporter. He was a banker and a merchant.

It is interesting to see how in the story in the present, the fairy works her way up the various deva (heavenly) realms appealing to the powers at be. But none of them can grant her forgiveness. She has to first earn the right to ask the Buddha and Anāthapiṇḍika for forgiveness.

"*I would rather plunge into the pit of coals.*" This story was told by the Master while at Jetavana. It is about Anāthapiṇḍika.

Anāthapiṇḍika had spent fifty-four crores (*one crore = 100,000 rupees, so 54 crores are 5,400,000 rupees*) on the Faith of the Buddha on the Monastery (*at Jetavana*). Nothing was more important to him than the Three Gems (*Buddha, Dharma, and Saṅgha*). He used to go to the monastery every day when the Master was at Jetavana to attend the Great Services: at daybreak, after breakfast, and in the evening. There were intermediate services too. But he never went empty-handed for fear that the novice monks and young lay disciples would see that he had not brought anything with him.

When he went in the early morning, he used to take rice with him. After breakfast he brought ghee, butter, honey, molasses, and the like. And in the evening, he brought perfumes, garlands and cloths. He spent so much every day that his expense knew no bounds.

At the same time, many traders borrowed money from him in the amount of eighteen crores (*1,800,000 rupees*), and the great merchant never called the money in. Furthermore, another eighteen crores of the family property, which were buried in the river bank, were washed out to sea when the bank was swept away by a storm. The money pots rolled down, with fastenings and seals unbroken, to the bottom of the ocean.

There was always enough rice in his house for 500 monks so that the merchant's house was to the Saṇgha like a water hole where four roads meet. He was like a mother and a father to them. Even the All-Enlightened Buddha used to go to his house and the Eighty Chief Elders, too, and the number of other monks passing in and out was beyond measure.

Now his house was seven stories high, and it had seven portals. There was a fairy who lived over the fourth gateway, and she was not a follower of the Buddha's teaching. When the All-Enlightened Buddha came into the house, she could not stay in her home on high, but she was required to come down with her children to the ground floor. She had to do the same thing whenever the Eighty Chief Elders or the other Elders came in and out. She thought to herself, "As long as the ascetic Gotama and his disciples keep coming into this house, I can have no peace here. I can't keep coming downstairs all the time to the ground floor. I must develop a scheme to stop them from coming any more to this house." So one day, when the business manager had retired to rest, she appeared before him in material form.

"Who is that?" he said.

"It is I," came the reply, "the fairy who lives over the fourth gateway."

"What brings you here?"

"You don't see what the merchant is doing. Disregarding his own future, he is spending all of his money to enrich the ascetic Gotama. He engages in no business. Tell the merchant to attend to his business and to stop the ascetic Gotama and his disciples from coming to the house anymore."

Then he said, "Foolish Fairy, if the merchant does spend his money, he spends it on the Faith of the Buddha. This leads to liberation. Even if he seizes me by the hair and sells me for a slave, I will say nothing. Go away!"

40: Khadiraṅgāra Jātaka,
The Pit of Coals

Another day, she went to the merchant's oldest son and gave him the same advice. He scoffed at her in the same way. But she did not dare to speak to the merchant on the matter.

Because of his unending generosity and not doing any business, the merchant's wealth began to disappear and his estate grew smaller and smaller, so that he sank slowly into poverty. His table, his dress, and his bed and food were no longer what they had once been. Yet, in spite of his new circumstances, he continued to take care of the Saṅgha even though he was no longer able to properly feed them.

So one day when he had bowed and taken his seat, the Master said to him, "Householder, are gifts being given at your house?"

"Yes, sir," he said, "But there's only a little sour porridge left over from yesterday."

"Do not be upset, householder, if you can only offer what is unpalatable. If your heart is good, the food that you give to Buddhas, Pacceka Buddhas, (*Pacceka means "solitary"*) and their disciples, will be good too. And why is this? Because of the greatness of the merit. Someone who makes his heart good cannot give a gift that is not good. This is demonstrated by the following passage:

> If the heart has faith, no gift is small
> To Buddhas or to their true disciples.
> It is said that no service is small
> That is paid to Buddhas, lords of great renown.
> Mark well the fruit that is rewarded from that poor gift
> Of porridge: dried-up, sour, and lacking salt.

Further, he said, "Householder, in giving this unpalatable gift, you are giving to those who have entered on the Noble Eightfold Path. I once stirred up all India by giving a great gift, and in my generosity and faith I poured forth as though I had made one mighty stream from the five great rivers. Yet I had not found anyone who had reached the Three Refuges or kept the Five Precepts. It is hard to find those who are worthy of offerings. Therefore, do not let your heart be troubled by the thought that your gift is unpalatable."

(*A gift made to followers of the Dharma has more merit than gifts given to those who do not follow the Dharma. The Buddha here is referring to a gift that he gave in a previous life to a Buddha even though there were no disciples.)*

Now that fairy who had not dared to speak to the merchant in the days of his generosity thought that he was now poor. And so, entering his bedroom at night she appeared before him in material form, standing in mid-air.

"Who's that?" the merchant said.

"I am the fairy, great merchant, who lives over the fourth gateway."

"What brings you here?"

"To give you counsel."

"Proceed, then."

"Great merchant, you are not thinking about your own future or for your own children. You have spent so much on the Faith of the ascetic Gotama without undertaking new business that you have been impoverished by the ascetic Gotama. But even in your poverty you do not abandon the ascetic Gotama! The monks are in and out of your house this very day just as usual! You cannot ever get back what they have taken. From now on you should not go to the ascetic Gotama and you should not let his disciples set foot inside your house. Do not even turn to look at the ascetic Gotama but attend to your trade and business in order to restore the family fortune."

Then he said to her, "Was this the counsel you wanted to give me?"

"Yes, it was."

The merchant, "The mighty Lord of Wisdom has protected me against a hundred, a thousand, even a hundred thousand fairies such as you! My faith is as strong and steadfast as Mount Sineru (*Meru*)! I have spent my effort on the faith that leads to liberation. Your words are wicked. They are a blow aimed at the Faith of the Buddhas by you, you wicked and impudent witch. I cannot live under the same roof with you. Leave my house and go live somewhere else!" Hearing these words of that devoted man and disciple, she could not stay. She went back to her dwelling, took her children by the hand, and left.

But even though she left, she thought that if she could not find a place to stay somewhere else, she could make her peace with the merchant and return to live in his house. With this in this mind she went to the

40: Khadiraṅgāra Jātaka,
The Pit of Coals

protector deity of the city and with due salutation stood in front of him. He asked her why she had come, and she said, "My lord, I spoke improperly to Anāthapiṇḍika, and in his anger he threw me out of my home. Take me to him and help us to reconcile so that he will let me live there again."

"But what did you say to the merchant?"

"I told him not to support the Buddha and the Saṅgha anymore and not to let the ascetic Gotama come to his house any more. This is what I said, my lord."

"Your words were wicked. It was a blow aimed at the Faith. I will not help you."

Getting no support from him, she went to the Four Great Regents of the world (*The Four Heavenly Kings, one for each direction*). And being rebuffed by them in the same way, she went on to Sakka, King of Devas. She told him her story, begging him still more earnestly: "Deva, finding no shelter, I wander about homeless, leading my children by the hand. Your majesty, please give me some place to live."

And he, too, said to her, "You have been wicked. It was a blow aimed at the Conqueror's Faith. I cannot speak to the merchant on your behalf. But I can tell you one way that the merchant might pardon you."

"Please tell me, deva."

"Men have borrowed eighteen crores from the merchant. Take his business agent, and without telling anybody go to their houses in the company of some young goblins. Stand in the middle of their houses with the promissory note in one hand and a receipt in the other and terrify them with your goblin power, saying, 'Here's an acknowledgment of the debt. Our merchant did not try to collect this debt while he was affluent. But now he is poor, and you must pay the money you owe.' By your goblin power collect all eighteen crores of gold and fill the merchant's empty treasuries. He had another treasure buried in the banks of the river Aciravatī, but when the bank was washed away, the treasure was swept into the sea. Get that back also by using your supernatural power and store it in his treasury. Further, there is another sum of eighteen crores lying unowned in such and such a place. Bring that too and pour the money into his empty treasury. When you have atoned for your wickedness by the recovery of these fifty-four crores, ask the merchant to forgive you."

Figure: Past Due Notice

"Very good, deva," she said. And she set to work obediently and did just as she had been told. When she had recovered all the money, she went into the merchant's bedroom at night and appeared before him in material form standing in the air.

The merchant asked who was there. She replied, "It is I, great merchant, the blind and foolish fairy who lived over your fourth gateway. In the stupidity of my folly I did not understand the virtue of a Buddha, and so I came to say what I said to you a few days ago. Please forgive my fault! At the direction of Sakka, King of Devas, I have atoned by recovering the eighteen crores owing to you, the eighteen crores that had been washed down into the sea, and another eighteen crores that were lying unowned in such and such a place. This makes fifty-four crores in all, which I have put into your empty treasury. The sum you spent on the Monastery at Jetavana is now

40: Khadiraṅgāra Jātaka,
The Pit of Coals

made up again. While I have nowhere to live, I am in misery. Please forgive my foolishness, great merchant, and pardon me."

Anāthapiṇḍika, hearing what she said, thought to himself, "She is a fairy, and she says she has atoned, and she confesses her fault. The Master will consider this and make his virtues known to her. I will take her before the All-Enlightened Buddha." So he said, "My good fairy, if you want me to pardon you, ask me in the presence of the master."

"Very good," she said, "I will. Take me along with you to the Master."

"Certainly," he said. And early in the morning, when night was just passing away, he took her with him to the Master and told the Blessed One all that she had done.

Hearing this, the Master said, "You see, householder, how the fool regards wickedness as excellent before it ripens to fruit. But when it does ripen, then he sees the wickedness to be wicked. Likewise, the good man looks on his goodness as unwholesome before it ripens to fruit. But when it ripens, he sees it to be goodness." And so saying, he repeated these two stanzas from the Dhammapada:

> The fool thinks his wicked deed is good
> As long as the wickedness has not ripened into fruit.
> But when the wickedness at last ripens,
> The fool sees "It was wicked what I did."

> The good man thinks his goodness is unwholesome
> As long as it has not ripened into fruit.
> But when his goodness begins to ripen,
> The good man surely sees "It was good that I did."

At the close of these stanzas that fairy was established in the Fruit of the First Path (*stream-entry*). She fell at the wheel-marked feet (*tradition holds that a Buddha has a Dharma wheel on the bottom of each foot*) of the Master, crying, "Blinded by passion, depraved by unskillfulness, misled by delusion, and blinded by ignorance, I spoke foolishly because I did not know your virtue. Please forgive me!" Then she was pardoned by the Master and the great merchant.

At this time Anāthapiṇḍika sang his own praises in the Master's presence, saying, "Sir, though this fairy did her best to stop me from giving support to the Buddha and his following, she did not succeed.

And though she tried to stop me from giving gifts, I still gave them! Was this not goodness on my part?"

The Master said, "You, householder, are a converted man and a good disciple. Your faith is firm and your vision is purified. It is not surprising that you were not stopped by this impotent fairy. The marvel was that the wise and good of a bygone day, when a Buddha had not appeared and when knowledge had not ripened to its full fruit, should give gifts from the heart of a lotus flower, even though Māra, lord of the Realm of Temptation, appeared in mid-heaven, shouting, 'If you give gifts, you will roast in hell,' showing them a pit eighty cubits deep filled with red-hot embers." And so saying, at the request of Anāthapiṇḍika, he told this story of the past.

Once upon a time when Brahmadatta was reigning in Benares, the Bodhisatta was born in the family of the Lord High Treasurer of Benares. He was raised in the lap of luxury like a royal prince. By the time he was sixteen years old, he had made himself perfect in all accomplishments. At his father's death he filled the office of Lord High Treasurer. He built six alms houses, one at each of the four gates of the city, one in the center of the city, and one at the gate of his own mansion. He was very generous, and he kept the precepts and observed the fasting days.

Now one day at breakfast time when wonderful food was being served to the Bodhisatta, a Pacceka Buddha arose after having been in deep meditation for seven days. Noticing that it was time to go on his alms rounds, he thought that it would be good to visit the Treasurer of Benares that morning. So he cleaned his teeth with a tooth-stick made from a betel vine, washed his mouth with water from Lake Anotatta, put on his inner robe as he stood on the tableland of Manosilā, fastened his outer robe, donned his upper robe, and took his alms bowl. He passed through the air and arrived at the gate of the mansion just as the Bodhisatta's breakfast was being served.

As soon as the Bodhisatta saw him, he rose from his seat and looked at the attendant, indicating that a service was required. "What would you like me to do, my lord?"

"Bring his reverence's bowl," the Bodhisatta said.

40: Khadiraṅgāra Jātaka,
The Pit of Coals

At that very instant Māra the Tempter rose up in a state of great excitement, saying, "It has been seven days since the Pacceka Buddha has eaten. If he does not get any food today, he will die. I will destroy him and stop the treasurer from giving anything."

And that very instant he conjured up a pit of red-hot embers inside the mansion, eighty cubits deep, filled with Acacia charcoal, all ablaze and aflame like the great hell of Avīci (*one of the hell realms*). When he had created this pit, Māra himself took his position in mid-air.

When the man who was on his way to fetch the bowl saw this, he was terrified and started back. "What makes you start back, my man?" asked the Bodhisatta.

"My lord," he answered, "there is a great pit of red-hot embers blazing and flaming in the middle of the house." And as man after man went to the spot, they were all panic-stricken and ran away as fast as their legs would carry them.

The Bodhisatta thought to himself, "Māra the Tempter must be trying to stop me from giving alms. I have yet to be, however, shaken by a hundred or by a thousand Maras. We will see whose strength is greater, whose might is mightier, mine or Māra's." So taking a bowl in his hand, he went to the fiery pit and looked up to the heavens. Seeing Māra, he said, "Who are you?"

"I am Māra," was the answer.

"Did you conjure this pit of red-hot embers?"

"Yes, I did."

"Why?"

"To stop you from giving alms and to destroy the life of that Pacceka Buddha."

"I will not permit you to stop me from giving alms or to destroy the life of the Pacceka Buddha. I am going to see today whether your strength or mine is greater."

And standing on the brink of that fiery pit, he cried, "Reverend Pacceka Buddha, even though I may fall headlong into this pit of red-hot embers, I will not turn back. Only promise to take the food I bring." And so saying he repeated this stanza:

I would rather plunge headlong
Into this gulf of hell then stoop to shame!
Promise me, sir, to take these alms from my hands!

With these words the Bodhisatta, grasping the bowl of food, strode on undaunted right onto the surface of the pit of fire. But even as he did so, there rose up to the surface through all the eighty cubits of the pit's depth a large and peerless lotus flower that grasped the feet of the Bodhisatta! And pollen fell from it onto the head of the Great Being, so that his whole body was sprinkled from head to foot with the dust of gold! Standing right in the heart of the lotus, he poured the precious food into the bowl of the Pacceka Buddha.

Figure: The Bodhisatta's Resolve

And when the latter had taken the food and given thanks, he flung his bowl up into the heavens, and right in everyone's sight he rose into the air and disappeared back to the Himalayas again, forming a track of fantastically shaped clouds in his path.

And Māra, too, defeated and dejected, passed away back to his home.

40: Khadiraṅgāra Jātaka,
The Pit of Coals

But the Bodhisatta, still standing in the lotus, taught the Dharma to the people, extolling alms-giving and the precepts, after which, surrounded by the escorting multitude, he went back into his mansion once more. And all his life he showed charity and did other good works until he passed away to fare according to his karma.

Said the Master, "It was no marvel, layman, that you, with your discernment of the Dharma, were not overcome by the fairy. The real marvel was what the wise and good did in bygone days." His lesson ended, the Master showed the connection and identified the birth by saying, "The Pacceka Buddha of those days passed away, never to be born again. I was the Treasurer of Benares who, defeating Māra and standing in the heart of the lotus, placed alms in the bowl of the Pacceka Buddha."

41: Losaka Jātaka,
The Story of Losaka

Both the story in the present and the Jātaka Tale are quite long. But as you read them, imagine that you are sitting around a campfire while someone tells the story.

There is something of mathematical interest in the story in the present, and that is how the villagers determine which family is causing their misfortune. They use a binary search, something well-known to people who work with computers. They keep diving their group in half until they know who is committing the offense.

It is also worth nothing Sāriputta's gentle compassion for Losaka. Even though Sāriputta is one of the most prominent people in the Buddha's Saṅgha, he acts as Losaka's humble servant in order to make sure he has a proper meal before he dies.

Also notice the behavior of the Elder. He is content to eat good food or not to eat at all. He sees that the monk is afraid that he will upstage the monk with the nobleman, so he chooses to stay at the monastery and meditate rather than infringe on the monk's territory. This is the behavior of an Arahat, someone who is kind and compassionate and is content to feed on the joy of meditation.

"The stubborn man." This story was told by the Master while at Jetavana. It is about the Elder Losaka Tissa.

"Who," you ask, "was this Elder Losaka Tissa?" Well, his father was a fisherman in Kosala, and he was the curse of his family. When he was a monk, no one gave him alms. When his previous existence ended, he had been conceived by a certain fisherman's wife in a fishing village of a thousand families in Kosala. And on the day he was conceived all those thousand families, with their fishing nets in hand, went fishing in the river, but they failed to catch one single fish. And that bad fortune plagued them from that day forward.

Before his birth, the village was destroyed seven times by fire, and it was attacked seven times by the King's vengeance. So in time the people fell into a woeful existence. Reflecting that it had not always been this way, and that now they were going to rack and ruin, they concluded that someone in their village was to blame. They decided

41: Losaka Jātaka,
The Story of Losaka

to divide into two groups. They did this, and this created two groups of five hundred families each. After that, misfortune came to the group that included the parents of the future Losaka, while the other five hundred families prospered. So the first group decided to go on dividing their group into two. They kept doing this until one family was separated from the rest. Then they knew that the cause of misfortune was in that family, and they drove them away.

It was very difficult for Losaka's mother to earn a living, but when her time came, she gave birth to her son. (He that is born into his last life cannot be killed. For like a lamp within a jar, the flame of destiny to become an Arahat burns so brightly inside of him.) The mother took care of the child until he could run about. When he could, she put a bowl in his hands and told him to go begging. When he did this, she ran away and abandoned him.

After that, the solitary child begged for his food and slept where he could. He was unwashed and bedraggled. He made a living like a mud-eating goblin (*a type of hungry ghost, beings that live one level below humans*). When he was seven years old, he was picking up and eating, like a crow, lump by lump, any rice he could find outside a house where they threw away the residue from the rice pots.

One day Sāriputta, Marshall of the Faith, went into Sāvatthi on his round for alms. He saw the child and wondered what village the hapless creature came from. He was filled with love for him and called out "Come here." The child came, bowed to the Elder, and stood before him. Then Sāriputta said, "What village do you belong to and where are your parents?"

"I am destitute, sir," the child said, "for my parents said they were exhausted, and so they abandoned me and went away."

"Would you like to become a monk?"

"Indeed, I should, sir. But who would take a poor wretch like me into the Saṅgha?"

"I will."

"Then, please let me become a monk."

The Elder gave the child a meal and took him to the monastery. He washed him with his own hands. He ordained him as a Novice first, and then gave him the full ordination later when he was old enough. In his old age he was known as Elder Losaka Tissa.

But he always suffered misfortune. Very little was given to him. The story goes that no matter how lavish the charity, he never got enough to eat. He only got enough to keep himself alive. A single ladle of rice appeared to fill his alms-bowl to the brim so that the person giving him food thought his bowl was full. Then they would give the rest of the rice to the next monk. When rice was being put into his bowl, it is said that the rice in the giver's dish would disappear. This happened with every kind of food. Even when he had attained awakening and won the highest Fruit of Arahatship, he still got little.

Eventually, when the karma of this existence was exhausted, the day came for him to pass away. As the Marshall of the Faith meditated, he became aware of this, and he thought to himself, "Losaka Tissa will pass away today, and today at least I will see that he has enough to eat." So he took the Elder and went to Sāvatthi for alms. But, because Losaka was with him, it was all in vain. When Sāriputta held out his hand for alms in the heavily populated Sāvatthi, he did not receive so much as a bow. So he told the Elder to go back and sit in the Dharma Hall of the Monastery. Then he collected food which he sent with a message that it was to be given to Losaka. Those to whom he gave the food took it, but, they forgot all about Losaka and ate it themselves. So when Sāriputta entered the monastery, Losaka came to him and saluted him. Sāriputta stopped and turned around and said, "Well, did you get the food, brother?"

"I shall, no doubt, get it in good time," the Elder said. Sāriputta was greatly troubled and looked to see what time it was. But noon had passed. (*Monastics are not allowed to eat solid food after noon.*) "Stay here, brother," Sāriputta said, "and do not move." He made Losaka Tissa sit down in the Dharma Hall and set out for the palace of the King of Kosala. The King commanded that his bowl be taken and saying that it was past noon and therefore not the time to eat rice, he ordered his bowl to be filled with the four sweet kinds of food. (*These are honey, ghee, butter, and sugar. The implication is that these are not considered solid food, so they can be eaten after noon.*). He returned with this and stood before Losaka, bowl in hand, and told the sage to eat. But because of the respect that he had for Sāriputta, the Elder was ashamed and would not eat. "Come, brother Tissa," Sāriputta said, "I must stand

41: Losaka Jātaka,
The Story of Losaka

with the bowl. Sit down and eat. If the bowl leaves my hand, everything in it will disappear."

So the venerable Elder Losaka Tissa ate the sweets while the exalted Marshall of the Faith stood holding the bowl. And thanks to the latter's virtue the food did not vanish. So the Elder Losaka Tissa ate as much as he wanted and was satisfied, and that same day he passed away to enter the realm of the Unconditioned, never to be born again.

The All-Enlightened Buddha stood by and saw the body cremated, and they built a stupa for the ashes.

Seated in the Dharma Hall, the monks said, "Monks, Losaka suffered from misfortune, and little was given to him. How is it possible that he could be so unfortunate yet he was still able to win the glory of Arahatship?"

Entering the Dharma Hall, the Master asked what they were talking about, and they told him. "Monks," he said, "this brother's past actions were the cause both of his receiving so little and of his becoming an Arahat. In bygone days he prevented others from receiving alms, and that is why he received so little himself. But it was by his meditating on suffering (*dukkha*), impermanence (*anicca*), and non-self (*anattā*) in all things, that he won Arahatship for himself." And so saying, he told this story of the past.

Once upon a time, in the days of the Buddha Kassapa (*the 27th of the previous 29 Buddhas named in the Canon*), there was a monk who lived the village life and was supported by a nobleman. He followed the monastic rules, he was virtuous in his life, and he overflowed with wisdom. There was also an Elder, an Arahat, who lived with his fellows in harmony. At the time of the story he visited the village where the nobleman who supported this monk lived.

The nobleman was so pleased with the demeanor of the Elder that he took his bowl, led him into the house, and with great respect invited him to eat. Then he listened to a short discourse by the Elder, and at its close he said with a bow, "Sir, please stay at our monastery close by. I will come and see you there in the evening."

So the Elder went to the monastery, saluted the resident monk on his arrival, and - after politely asking permission - took a seat by his side.

The monk received him with great friendliness and asked him whether he had been given any food as alms.

"Oh yes," replied the Elder.

"Where was it?"

"Why, in your village close by, at the nobleman's house."

And so saying, the Elder asked to be shown to his room and made it ready. Then laying aside his bowl and robe and seating himself, he became absorbed in deep meditation.

In the evening the nobleman came with servants carrying flowers and perfumes and lamps and oil. Saluting the resident monk, he asked whether a guest had appeared, an Elder. Being told that he had, the nobleman asked where he was and in what room he was staying. Then the nobleman went to the Elder and, after bowing courteously, seated himself next to the Elder and listened to a discourse. In the cool of the evening the nobleman made his offerings at the stupa and the Bodhi tree (*many monasteries in India had Bodhi trees that were propagated from a cutting of the original Bodhi tree*), lit his lamp, and left after inviting both Elder and monk to come up to his house the next day for their meal.

"I'm losing my hold on the nobleman," the monk thought. "If this Elder stays here, I will count for nothing with him." So he was discontented and started scheming how to convince the Elder not to settle down there for good. When the Elder came to pay his respects in the early morning, the monk did not speak. The Arahat read his mind and said to himself, "This monk does not know that I would never stand between him and the family that supports him or his Sangha." And going back to his room, he became absorbed in deep meditation.

On the next day, the resident monk, having first knocked gently on the gong, went off alone to the nobleman's house. Taking his alms-bowl from him, the nobleman told him to be seated and asked where the stranger was.

"I have no news of your friend," said the monk. "Even though I knocked on the gong and tapped at his door, I couldn't wake him. I can only presume that his rich food here yesterday disagreed with him and that he is still in bed as a result."

41: Losaka Jātaka,
The Story of Losaka

Meantime the Arahat, who had waited until the proper time to go on his alms round, had washed and dressed and risen with his bowl and robe and gone elsewhere.

The nobleman gave the monk rice and milk to eat, with ghee and sugar and honey in it. Then he had his bowl scoured with perfumed soap and filled it again, saying, "Sir, the Elder must be tired from his trip. Take this to him."

Figure: The Wicked Act

Without hesitation the monk took the food and went on his way. He thought to himself, "If our friend tastes this, even if I take him by the throat and kick him out of doors I won't get rid of him. But how can I get rid of this food? If I give it to someone, it will be discovered. If I throw it into the water, the ghee will float on top. And if I throw it on the ground, that will only bring all the crows of the district flocking to the spot." In his bewilderment he saw a field that had been burned (*this is still done to improve fertility*), and, scraping away the embers, he threw the contents of his bowl into the hole, filled in the embers on the top, and went home. Not finding the Elder there, he thought that the Arahat had understood his jealousy and departed. "Woe is me," he cried, "for my greed has made me act wickedly."

From then on misfortune fell on him and he became like a living ghost. He died soon after and was reborn in hell. He was tormented there for hundreds of thousands of years. Because of his karma, he was an ogre for five hundred consecutive births. He never had enough to eat, except one day when he enjoyed an abundance of decaying animal flesh.

* * *

For the next five hundred existences he was a dog. Here, too, he only had enough to eat on one day. On no other occasion did he have enough to eat. Even when he stopped being reborn as a dog, he was born into a beggar family in a Kāsi village. From the hour of his birth, that family became even more impoverished, and he never got half as much gruel as he wanted. And he was called Mittavindaka (*friend who suffers*).

Finally, unable to endure the pangs of hunger that now beset them, his father and mother beat him and drove him away, crying, "Go away, you curse!"

In the course of his travels, the little outcast came to Benares. In those days the Bodhisatta was a world-renowned teacher with five hundred young brahmins to teach. In those times the people of Benares gave food to poor young men and had them taught for free. So Mittavindaka also became a charity scholar under the Bodhisatta. But he was fierce and stubborn, always fighting with the other students and heedless of his master's criticism. As a result, the Bodhisatta's income fell off.

Because he quarreled so much and would not accept criticism, the youth ended up running away. He came to a border-village where he hired himself out in order to earn a living. He married a miserably poor woman with whom he had two children. Later, the villagers paid him to teach them what was true Dharma and what was false. They gave him a hut to live in at the entrance to their village. But because of Mittavindaka's coming to live with them, the King's vengeance fell on

41: Losaka Jātaka,
The Story of Losaka

those villagers seven times, and seven times their homes were burned to the ground. And seven times their water tank dried up.

Then they discussed the situation and agreed that things had not been this bad before Mittavindaka came to live there, but that ever since he came things had gone from bad to worse. So with blows they drove him from their village. He left with his family and came to a haunted forest. There the demons killed and ate his wife and children. Fleeing once again, after many days he came to a village on the coast called Gambhīra. He arrived on a day when a ship was putting to sea, and he signed on to the ship's crew. For a week the ship sailed on her way, but on the seventh day she was becalmed in mid-ocean. It was as though she had run aground on a rock. Then they cast lots in order to determine who was the cause of their trouble. Seven times in a row the lot fell on Mittavindaka. So they gave him a raft of bamboo and threw him overboard. And with that, the ship made way again.

Mittavindaka clambered on to his bamboo raft and floated on the waves. Thanks to his having obeyed the monastic rules in the time of the Buddha Kassapa, he found four daughters of the gods living in a palace of crystal in mid-ocean. He lived happily there for seven days.

Now palace ghosts only enjoy happiness for seven days at a time. So when the seventh day came and they had to go to their punishment, they left him with instructions to wait for their return. But no sooner had they left than Mittavindaka left on his raft again and went to where eight daughters of the gods lived in a palace of silver. Leaving them in turn, he went to where 16 daughters of the gods lived in a palace of jewels, and after that to where 32 lived in a palace of gold.

Disregarding their instructions, he again sailed away and came to a city of ogres set among islands. There an ogress was ranging about in the shape of a goat. Not knowing that she was an ogress, Mittavindaka thought he could make a meal of the goat, and he grabbed the creature by the leg. Immediately, by virtue of her demon-nature, she threw him up and over the ocean. He landed on a thorn bush on the slopes of the dry moat of Benares and then rolled down to earth.

Now it happened that at that time thieves used to frequent that moat and kill the King's goats, and the goatherds had determined to catch the rascals. Mittavindaka picked himself up and saw the goats. He thought to himself, "Well, it was a goat on an island in the ocean that threw me over the sea when I seized it by the leg. Perhaps, if I do this to one of these goats, I may get thrown back again to where the daughters of the gods live in their ocean palaces." So without thinking, he grabbed one of the goats by the leg. At once the goat began to bleat, and the goatherds came running from every side. They grabbed hold of him at once, crying, "This is the thief that has so lived so long on the King's goats." And they beat him and began to drag him away in chains to the King.

Just then the Bodhisatta, with his 500 young brahmins around him, was coming out of the city to bathe. Seeing and recognizing Mittavindaka, he said to the goatherds, "Why, this is a pupil of mine, my good men. Why have you seized him?"

"Master," they said, "we caught this thief in the act of seizing a goat by the leg, and that's why we've got hold of him."

"Well," the Bodhisatta said, "suppose you hand him over to us to live with us as our slave."

"All right, sir," the men replied. And letting their prisoner go, they went their way. Then the Bodhisatta asked Mittavindaka where he had been all that time, and Mittavindaka told him all that had happened.

"It is through not heeding those who wished him well," said the Bodhisatta, "that he suffered all these misfortunes." And he recited this stanza:

> *The stubborn man who, when exhorted, pays*
> *No heed to friends who kindly give advice,*
> *Shall come to certain harm, like Mittaka,*
> *When he seized the grazing goat by the leg.*

And after a time both the Teacher and Mittavindaka passed away to fare according to their karma.

The Master said, "This Losaka was both the cause of his getting little and of his attaining Arahatship." His lesson ended, he showed the connection and identified the birth by saying, "The Elder Losaka Tissa was the Mittavindaka of those days, and I was the Teacher of worldwide fame."

42: Kapota Jātaka, *The Greedy Crow*

This is a warning story about the dangers of greed. One lovely detail is that the people of Benares had a custom of putting up baskets for the "shelter and comfort of the birds."

A less appealing detail in the story is that the chef could have simply killed the crow, but instead he decided to torture him. Yikes!

"The headstrong man." This story was told by the Master while at Jetavana. It is about a certain greedy monk. His greediness will be related in the Sixth Book in the Kāka Jātaka (*Jātaka* 395).

But on this occasion the monks said to the Master, "Sir, this monk is greedy."

The Master said, "Is it true what they say, brother, that you are greedy?"

"Yes, sir," he replied.

"So too in bygone days, brother, you were greedy, and because of your greediness, you lost your life. You also caused the wise and good to lose their home." And so saying he told this story of the past.

Once upon a time when Brahmadatta was reigning in Benares, the Bodhisatta was born as a pigeon. Now the Benares people of those days, as an act of goodness, used to hang up straw baskets in various places for the shelter and comfort of the birds. And the cook of the Lord High Treasurer of Benares hung up one of these baskets in his kitchen. The Bodhisatta took up residence there, leaving at daybreak in search of food, and returning home in the evening. And so he lived his life.

But one day a crow, flying over the kitchen, smelled the wonderful aroma of the salt and fresh fish and meat there, and he was filled with longing to taste it. While he was pondering how to do this, he perched nearby, and in the evening he saw the Bodhisatta come home and go into the kitchen. "Ah!" he thought, "I can manage it through the pigeon."

So he came back the next day at dawn, and, when the Bodhisatta left in search of food, he following him around from place to place like his shadow. So the Bodhisatta said, "Why are you following me, friend?"

"My lord," answered the crow, "I admire your demeanor, and from now on I want to follow you."

"But friend, your kind of food and mine is not the same," the Bodhisatta said. "It will be difficult for you if you attach yourself to me."

"My lord," said the crow, "when you are looking for your food, I will feed too, by your side."

"So be it, then," the Bodhisatta said. "However, you must be sincere." And with this warning to the crow, the Bodhisatta flew about pecking up grass seed, while the crow went about turning over cow dung and picking out the insects underneath until he was full.

When the Bodhisatta had eaten and reached home again in the evening, the crow flew in with him into the kitchen.

"Why, our bird has brought another one home with him," exclaimed the cook, and he hung up a second basket for the crow. And from that time onward the two birds lived together in the kitchen.

Now one day the Lord High Treasurer brought in a store of fish which the cook hung up about the kitchen. Filled with a burning desire at the sight, the crow made up his mind to stay at home the next day and treat himself to this excellent fare.

So all the night long he lay groaning, and on the next day, when the Bodhisatta was about to leave in search of food, he said, "Come along, friend crow." The crow replied, "Go without me, my lord, for I have a pain in my stomach."

"Friend," the Bodhisatta answered, "I have never heard of crows having pains in their stomachs before. True, crows feel faint in each of the three night-watches (*in India they divided the night into three "watches"*), but if they eat a lamp wick, this calms their hunger. You must be yearning for the fish in the kitchen here. Come now, man's food will not agree with you. Do not behave like this. Come and find your food with me."

"Indeed, I am not able to, my lord," the crow said.

42: Kapota Jātaka,
The Greedy Crow

"Well, your true nature will show," said the Bodhisatta. "But do not give in to greed. Be steadfast." And with this admonition, he flew away to find his daily food.

Meanwhile the cook took several kinds of fish and dressed some one way and some another. Then lifting the lids off his sauce pans a little to let the steam out, he put a colander on the top of one and went outside the door. He stood there wiping the sweat from his brow. Just at that moment the crow's head popped out from the basket. A glance told him that the cook was away, and he thought, "It is now or never. The only question is should I take chopped meat or a big lump?" Thinking that it takes a long time to make a full meal of chopped meat, he decided to take a large piece of fish and sit and eat it in his basket. So he flew out and landed on the colander. "Click" went the colander.

Figure: The Greedy Crow is Caught!

"What can that be?" the cook said, running in on hearing the noise. Seeing the crow, he cried, "Oh, there's that rascally crow wanting to eat my master's dinner. I have to work for my master, not for that rascal! What's he to me, I should like to know?" So he shut the door, caught the crow, and plucked every feather off his body. Then he pounded up ginger with salt and cumin and mixed in sour buttermilk, soaked the crow in the pickle, and threw him back into his basket. And there the crow lay groaning, overcome by the agony of his pain.

In the evening the Bodhisatta came back and saw the wretched plight of the crow. "Ah! greedy crow," he exclaimed, "you would not listen to my advice, and now your own greed has caused you trouble." So saying, he repeated this stanza:

> The headstrong man who, when warned, pays
> No heed to friends who kindly give advice,
> Shall surely perish, like the greedy crow,
> Who laughed to scorn the pigeon's warning words.

Then, exclaiming "I too can no longer live here," the Bodhisatta flew away. But the crow died then and there, and the cook flung him, basket and all, on the dust-heap.

The Master said, "You were greedy, brother, in bygone times, just as you are now. And because of your greediness the wise and good of those days had to abandon their homes." Having ended this lesson, the Master preached the Four Noble Truths, at the close of which that monk won the Fruit of the Second Path (*once returner*). Then the Master showed the connection and identified the birth as follows, "The greedy brother was the crow of those times, and I was the pigeon."

43: Veḷuka Jātaka,
Bamboo's Father

This is part of the "headstrong and stubborn series" of Jātaka Tales, this being the third story in a row with this theme. In this story a monk takes the Buddhist compassion for animals and puts a practical spin on it. You can befriend certain animals – and people – and you can have compassion for them and love them, but you should not necessarily trust them. This story could also be called, "It is good to be kind but let's not get carried away."

"The headstrong man." This story was told by the Master while at Jetavana. It is about a certain headstrong monk. For the Blessed One asked him whether it was true that he was headstrong, and the monk admitted that he was. "Brother," said the Master, "this is not the first time you have been headstrong. You were just as headstrong in former days. And as the result of your stubborn refusal to follow the advice of the wise and good, you were killed by the bite of a snake." And so saying, he told this story of the past.

Once upon a time when Brahmadatta was reigning in Benares, the Bodhisatta was born into a wealthy family in the Kingdom of Kāsi. Having come to years of discretion, he saw how pain springs from passion and how true bliss comes by abandoning of passion. So he abandoned lust and went to the Himalayas to became a recluse. There he won by mastering the ordained mystic meditations the five orders of the Higher Knowledge (*presumably the "five trainee's powers", i.e., the power of faith, the power of moral shame, the power of moral dread, the power of energy, and the power of wisdom*) and the eight Attainments (*the 8 jhānas*). And because he lived his life in the rapture of insight, he came to have a large following of five hundred recluses, and he was their teacher.

Now one day a young poisonous viper, wandering about as vipers do, came to the hut of one of the hermits. And that monk grew as fond of the creature as if it were his own child. He housed it in a piece of bamboo and showed kindness to it. And because it was lodged in a piece of bamboo, the viper was known by the name of "Bamboo." Moreover, because the monk was so fond of the viper and because he treated it as if it were his own child, they called him "Bamboo's Father."

Hearing that one of the monks was keeping a viper, the Bodhisatta sent for that monk and asked him whether this was true. When told that it was true, the Bodhisatta said, "A viper can never be trusted. Do not keep it any longer."

"But," pleaded the monk, "my viper is as dear to me as a pupil to a teacher. I could not live without him."

"Well then," the Bodhisatta answered, "know that this very snake will lose you your life." But heedless of the master's warning, that monk still kept the pet he could not bear to part with.

A very few days later all the monks went out to gather fruits. They came to a spot where all kinds grew bountifully, so they stayed there two or three days. "Bamboo's Father" went with them, leaving his viper behind in his bamboo prison. Two or three days afterwards, when he came back, he went to feed the creature. Opening the cane, he stretched out his hand, saying, "Come, my son. You must be hungry." But the viper was angry because he had not eaten, so the viper bit his outstretched hand, killing him on the spot, and then escaped into the forest.

Figure: Biting the Hand That Feeds You

43: Veḷuka Jātaka,
Bamboo's Father

Seeing him lying there dead, the monks came and told the Bodhisatta. He told them to cremate the body. Then, seated in their midst, he exhorted the monks by repeating this stanza:

The headstrong man, who, when exhorted, pays
No heed to friends who kindly give their counsel,
Like 'Bamboo's father,' they shall come to nothing.

Thus did the Bodhisatta exhort his followers, and he developed within himself the four Noble States (*the first four jhānas*), and at his death he was reborn into the Brahma Realm.

The Master said, "Brother, this is not the first time you have been headstrong. You were just as stubborn in times gone by, and because of it you met your death from a viper's bite." Having ended his lesson, the Master showed the connection and identified the birth by saying, "In those days, this headstrong monk was 'Bamboo's Father,' my disciples were the band of recluses, and I was their teacher."

44: Makasa Jātaka,
The Mosquito

This story sounds more like an episode of The Three Stooges than a morality tale. This would be a fun story to tell to a child.

There is a lot of humor in the Pāli Canon, although some of it is quite subtle. Ṭhānissaro Bhikkhu has written a book about it. It is called "The Buddha Smiles: Humor in the Pāli Canon."

"Friends who lack sense." This story was told by the Master while on an alms pilgrimage in Magadha. It is about some stupid villagers in a certain town. Tradition says that, after travelling from Sāvatthi to the kingdom of Magadha, he was on his alms round in that kingdom when he arrived at the town. This town was filled with fools. These fools met together one day and said, "Friends, when we are at work in the jungle, the mosquitoes devour us and that hinders our work. Let us arm ourselves with bows and weapons, go to war with the mosquitoes, and shoot or hack them all to death." So off they went to the jungle, shouting, "Shoot down the mosquitoes!" Unfortunately, they shot and struck each other until they were in a sad state. They returned only to sink on the ground in the village or at its entrance.

Surrounded by the Saṅgha, the Master went to that village for alms. The sensible minority among the inhabitants no sooner saw the Blessed One then they erected a pavilion at the entrance to their village. After giving large alms to the monks with the Buddha at its head, they bowed to the Master and seated themselves. Seeing wounded men lying around on this side and that, the Master asked those lay people, "There are many disabled men about. What happened to them?"

"Sir," they replied, "they went to war with the mosquitoes, but only shot one another and hurt themselves."

The Master said, "This is not the first time that these foolish people have injured themselves instead of the mosquitoes they meant to kill. In former times, also, there were those who, meaning to hit a mosquito, hit a fellow creature instead." And so saying, at the villagers' request he told this story of the past.

44: Makasa Jātaka,
The Mosquito

Once upon a time when Brahmadatta was reigning in Benares, the Bodhisatta earned his livelihood as a trader. In those days in a border village in Kāsi there were many carpenters. And it so happened that one of them, a bald grey-haired man, was planing away at some wood with his head glistening like a copper bowl, when a mosquito landed on his scalp and stung him with its dart-like sting.

The carpenter said to his son, who was seated nearby, "My boy, there's a mosquito stinging me on the head. Do drive it away."

"Hold still then, father," said the son, "one blow will settle it."

(At that very time the Bodhisatta had reached that village in the way of trade and was sitting in the carpenter's shop.)

"Rid me of it," cried the father.

"All right, father," the son answered. From behind the old man's back, he raised a sharp axe on high intending to kill the mosquito. But he split his father's head in two, and the old man fell dead on the spot.

Figure: "Hold still. I've got this."

The Bodhisatta, who had been an eye-witness to the whole scene, thought, "It is better to have an enemy with sense then a friend like that. At least an enemy will be deterred from killing because of the fear of vengeance." And he recited these lines:

> *Friends who lack sense are worse than enemies with sense.*
> *Witness the son that sought to kill the gnat,*
> *But split, poor fool, his father's skull in two.*

So saying, the Bodhisatta rose up and departed, passing away in after days to fare according to his karma. And as for the carpenter, his body was cremated by his kinsfolk.

"Thus, lay people," the Master said, "in bygone times there also were those who, seeking to hit a mosquito, struck down another person." This lesson ended, he showed the connection and identified the birth by saying, "In those days I was myself the wise and good trader who departed after repeating the stanza."

45: Rohiṇī Jātaka,
Rohiṇī's Tale

This story is almost identical to the previous one, but this one has a mother and daughter rather than a father and son.

Both stories emphasize that a worthy enemy is often less dangerous than a friend who lacks good sense. And if you think about all the times that "friends" talk someone into doing something stupid, or all the times that friends are a bad influence, this makes sense. There are many passages in the Pāli Canon that emphasize the importance of good friendship. And likewise, in one passage the Buddha says that if you cannot find good friends, you are better off being alone:

> If, while on your way,
> > You meet no one your equal or better,
> Steadily continue on your way alone.
> > There is no fellowship with fools.
> - [Dhp 61]

"*Friends who lack sense.*" This story was told by the Master while at Jetavana. It is about a maid servant of the Lord High Treasurer, Anāthapiṇḍika. For he is said to have had a maid servant named Rohiṇī. Her aged mother came to where the girl was pounding rice and lay down. The flies came flying all around the old woman and stung her as with a needle, so she cried to her daughter, "The flies are stinging me, my dear. Do drive them away."

"Oh! I'll drive them away, mother," said the girl, lifting her pestle up to swat the flies that had settled on her mother. Then, crying, "I'll kill them!", she hit her mother so hard that she killed the old woman outright. Seeing what she had done the girl began to weep and cry, "Oh! mother, mother!"

The news was brought to the Lord High Treasurer, who, after having the body cremated, went to the monastery. There he told the Master what had happened. "This is not the first time, layman," said the Master, "that in Rohiṇī's haste to kill the flies on her mother, she has struck her mother dead with a pestle. She did exactly the same in times past." Then at Anāthapiṇḍika's request, he told this story of the past.

Jātaka Tales

Once upon a time when Brahmadatta was reigning in Benares, the Bodhisatta was born as the son of the Lord High Treasurer. When the Lord High Treasurer died, he himself became the Lord High Treasurer. And he, too, had a maid servant whose name was Rohiṇī. And her mother, in like manner, went to where the daughter was pounding rice, and lay down, and called out, "Do drive these flies off me, my dear." And in just the same way she struck her mother with a pestle, and killed her, and began to weep.

Figure: Guilty, Guilty, Guilty!

Hearing what had happened, the Bodhisatta reflected: "Here, in this world, even an enemy, with sense, would be preferable," and he recited these lines:

Friends who lack sense are worse than enemies with sense,
Witness the girl whose reckless hand laid low
Her mother, who she now laments in vain.

In these lines in praise of the wise, the Bodhisatta taught the Dharma.

45: Rohiṇī Jātaka,
Rohiṇī's Tale

"This is not the first time, lay people," the Master said, "that in Rohiṇī's haste to kill flies she has killed her own mother instead." This lesson ended, he showed the connection and identified the birth by saying: "The mother and daughter of today were also mother and daughter of those bygone times, and I myself was the Lord High Treasurer."

46: Ārāmadūsaka Jātaka, *The Garden Spoiler*

The theme of this story is something akin to "the road to hell is paved with good intentions." We do a great deal of harm because of a lack of wisdom, like giving money to an alcoholic who just runs straight to the liquor store.

The Buddha's path is not "good intentions," it is wise and skillful intentions. If we act from our emotions rather than from intelligence and wisdom, we can do a great deal of harm.

"It is knowledge." The Master told this story in a certain village of Kosala. It is about someone who spoiled a pleasure garden.

Tradition says that, in the course of an alms journey among the people of Kosala, the Master came to a certain village. A wealthy landowner invited the Buddha to eat the midday meal at his house. He had his guest seated in the pleasure garden. There he showed hospitality to the Saṅgha with the Buddha at its head, and he courteously gave them permission to stroll about the grounds. So the monks rose up and walked about the grounds with the gardener. Observing a bare space in their walk, they said to the gardener, "Lay disciple, there is abundant shade everywhere else in the pleasure garden, but here there is neither tree nor shrub. Why is that?"

"Sirs," the man replied, "when these grounds were being laid out, a village lad, who was doing the watering, pulled up all the young trees and then gave them too much or too little water according to the size of their roots. So the young trees withered and died, and that is why this space is bare."

Going back to the Master, the monks told him this. "Yes, monks," he said, "this is not the first time that village lad has spoiled a pleasure garden. He did the same thing in bygone times as well." And so saying, he told this story of the past.

Once upon a time when Brahmadatta was the King of Benares, a festival was proclaimed in the city. At the first summoning notes of the festival drum, the towns people poured out to keep holiday.

Now in those days, a tribe of monkeys was living in the King's pleasure garden. The King's gardener thought to himself, "They are having a holiday in the city. I'll get the monkeys to do the watering for

46: Ārāmadūsaka Jātaka,
The Garden Spoiler

me and go off to enjoy myself with everyone else." So saying, he went to the king of the monkeys. He discussed how much they benefited from living in the pleasure garden because of the flowers and fruit and young shoots to eat. He ended by saying, "Today there is a holiday in the city, and I'm going off to enjoy it myself. Couldn't you water the young trees while I'm away?"

"Oh! yes," said the monkey.

"Only mind that you do," said the gardener; and off he went, giving the monkeys water skins and wooden watering pots to do the work.

The monkeys took the water skins and watering pots and started to water the young trees. "But we must be careful not to waste the water," observed their monkey king. As you water, first pull each young tree up and look at the size of its roots. Then give plenty of water to those whose roots are deep, but only give a little to those with tiny roots. When this water is all gone, it will be difficult to get more."

"We will," said the other monkeys, and they did as he had instructed them.

Figure: The Foolish Monkey

At this point a certain wise man, seeing what the monkeys were doing, asked why they pulled up tree after tree and watered them according to the size of their roots.

"Because this was our King's command," the monkeys answered.

Their reply moved the wise man to consider how, with every desire to do good, the ignorant and foolish only succeed in doing harm. And he recited this stanza:

> *It is knowledge that crowns effort with success,*
> *For fools are thwarted by their foolishness,*
> *--Witness the ape that killed the garden trees.*

With this rebuke to the king of the monkeys, the wise man departed from the pleasure garden with his followers.

The Master said, "This is not the first time, monks, that this village lad has spoiled a pleasure garden. He did the same thing in bygone times as well." His lesson ended, he showed the connection and identified the birth by saying, "The village lad who spoiled this pleasure garden was the king of the monkeys in those days, and I was the wise and good man."

47: Vāruṇi Jātaka,
The Liquor Spoiler

This is another curious story that presumably is a folk tale borrowed and inserted into a Buddhist context. Like the last story, it is about foolish, unskillful behavior done from a desire to do good.

What makes this story curious is that in the Buddha's teaching, selling alcohol is one of the jobs from which Buddhist laypeople are forbidden. And in the Five Precepts the fifth Precept is against the consumption of alcohol.

"*It is knowledge.*" This story was told by the Master while at Jetavana. It is about one who spoiled liquor. Tradition says that Anāthapiṇḍika had a friend who kept a tavern. This friend had a supply of strong liquor that he sold for gold and for silver, and his tavern was crowded. He gave orders to his apprentice to sell for cash only, and he went off to bathe. This apprentice, while serving out the alcohol to his customers, saw them sending out for salt and brown sugar and eating it as an appetizer. He thought to himself, "There must not be any salt in our liquor. I'll put some in." So he put a pound of salt in a bowl of the liquor, and he served it to the customers. As soon as they drank it, they spit it out again, saying, "What did you do?"

"I saw you sending for salt after drinking our liquor, so I mixed some salt in."

"And that's how you have spoiled good liquor, you idiot," cried the customers, and with abuse they got up one after another and left the tavern. When the keeper of the tavern came home and did not see a single customer, he asked where they had all gone. So the apprentice told him what had happened. Berating him for his folly, the man went off and told Anāthapiṇḍika. And the latter, thinking the story a good one to tell, went to Jetavana. There, after paying his respects, he told the Master all about it.

"This is not the first time, layman," the Master said, "that this apprentice has spoiled liquor. He did the same once before." Then at Anāthapiṇḍika's request, he told this story of the past.

Once upon a time when Brahmadatta was reigning in Benares, the Bodhisatta was the Treasurer of Benares, and he had a tavern keeper who lived under his protection. This man acquired a supply of strong spirits, which he left his apprentice to sell while he himself went off to bathe. During his absence his apprentice mixed salt with the liquor and spoiled it just in the same way. When he returned the young man's guide and master found out what had happened. Later he told the story to the Treasurer. "Truly," said the Treasurer, "the ignorant and foolish, with every desire to do good, only succeed in doing harm." And he recited this stanza:

> *It is knowledge that crowns our efforts with success;*
> *For fools are thwarted by their foolishness.*
> *Witness the tavern's salted bowl of liquor.*

In these lines the Bodhisatta taught the truth.

Figure: The Terrible Bartender

47: Vāruṇi Jātaka,
The Liquor Spoiler

The Master said, "Layman, this same person spoiled liquor in the past as now." Then he showed the connection and identified the birth by saying, "He who spoiled the liquor now was also the spoiler of the liquor in those bygone days, and I myself was then the Treasurer of Benares."

48: Vedabbha Jātaka,
The Treasure Spell

This is one of the longer stories, and it has two themes. One is someone who is intelligent but is too stubborn to accept wise advice. The original translation uses the word "self-willed," which I have changed to "headstrong."

The other theme is greed. And the story has a poignant lesson about how greed can go terribly wrong.

"Misguided effort." The Master told this story while at Jetavana. It is about a headstrong monk. The Master said to that monk, "This is not the first time, brother, that you have been headstrong. You had the same disposition in bygone times. You would not follow the advice of the wise and good. As a result, you were the cause for a thousand men to meet their end. And you were cut in two by a sharp sword and thrown on the highway." And so saying, he told this story of the past.

Once upon a time when Brahmadatta was reigning in Benares, there was a brahmin in a village who knew a magic spell called "Vedabbha." Now this spell, so they say, was precious beyond all measure. For at a certain conjunction of the planets, if the spell was repeated while looking upwards to the skies, the Seven Things of Worth - gold, silver, pearl, coral, catseye, ruby, and diamond – rained from the heavens.

In those days the Bodhisatta was a pupil of this brahmin. One day his master took the Bodhisatta with him and left the village to go to the country of Ceti.

Along the road to Ceti there was a forest. And in this forest there were five hundred robbers known as "the Dispatchers." They made it impossible to pass through. And these robbers caught the Bodhisatta and the Vedabbha-brahmin.

(Why, you might ask, were they called "the Dispatchers?" Well, the story goes that for every two prisoners they caught, they used to dispatch one to fetch the ransom. So that is why they were called "the Dispatchers." If they captured a father and a son, they told the father to go for the ransom to free his son. If they caught a mother and her daughter, they sent the mother for the money. If they caught two

48: Vedabbha Jātaka,
The Treasure Spell

brothers, they let the elder brother go, and if they caught a teacher and his student, they sent the student. In this case, therefore, they kept the Vedabbha-brahmin, and sent the Bodhisatta for the ransom.)

The Bodhisatta bowed to his Master and said, "In a day or two I will surely be back. Have no fear, but heed my advice. Today is the conjunction of the planets that brings about the rain of the Things of Worth. Do not repeat the spell and call down the precious shower. For if you do, calamity will come both to you and this band of robbers." With this warning to his master, the Bodhisatta left to get the ransom.

At sunset the robbers tied the brahmin up and shackled his feet. Just at this moment the full moon rose over the eastern horizon, and the brahmin, studying the heavens, knew that the great conjunction was taking place. "Why," he thought, "should I suffer this misery? If I repeat the spell I will call down the precious rain, pay the robbers the ransom, and go free." So he called out to the robbers, "Friends, why did you take me a prisoner?"

"To get a ransom, reverend sir," they said.

"Well, if that is all you want," the brahmin said, "then untie me, wash my head, put clean clothes on me, put perfume on me, and put garlands of flowers on me. Then leave me alone."

The robbers did as he asked. And the brahmin, marking the conjunction of the planets, repeated his spell with eyes lifted up to the heavens. Immediately the Things of Worth poured down from the skies! The robbers picked them all up and wrapped their treasure into bundles with their cloaks. Then they marched away with the brahmin following in the rear.

However, as luck would have it, the party was captured by a second band of five hundred robbers! "Why do you seize us?" said the first to the second band.

"For treasure," they answered.

"If you want treasure, seize that brahmin. He can bring riches down like rain from the skies by simply gazing upwards. He gave us everything that we have."

So the second band of robbers let the first band go, and they seized the brahmin, crying, "Give us riches too!"

Jātaka Tales

Figure: Raining Treasure

"It would give me great pleasure," the brahmin said, "but it will be a year before the conjunction of the planets takes place again. If you will only wait until then, I will summon the precious shower for you."

"You rascal brahmin!" the angry robbers cried. "You made the other band rich immediately, but you want us to wait a whole year!" And with that they cut him in two with a sharp sword and threw his body into the middle of the road.

Then they chased down the first band of robbers. They killed every one of them in hand-to-hand combat, and then they seized the treasure. Next, they divided themselves into two companies and fought among themselves, company against company, until two hundred and fifty of them were killed. And so they went on killing one another until only two of them were left alive. Thus did those thousand men come to destruction.

Now, when the two survivors had carried off the treasure, they hid it in the jungle near a village. One of them sat there, sword in hand, to guard it, while the other one went into the village to get rice and have it cooked for supper.

"Greed is the root of ruin!" thought the man who was guarding the treasure. "When my mate comes back, he will want half of this.

48: Vedabbha Jātaka,
The Treasure Spell

Suppose I kill him the moment he gets back." So he drew his sword and sat waiting for his comrade's return.

Meanwhile, the other man had reflected in the same way that the treasure had to be shared, and he thought to himself, "Suppose I poison the rice and keep the whole treasure to myself." So when the rice was boiled, he ate his own share, and then put poison in the rest. Then he carried it back with him to the jungle. But as soon as he set the rice down, the other robber cut him in two with his sword and hid the body in a secluded spot. Then he ate the poisoned rice and died right then and there. Thus, because of the treasure, the brahmin and all of the robbers came to destruction.

After a day or two the Bodhisatta came back with the ransom. He did not find his master where he had left him, but he did see the treasure strewn all about. His heart sank as he thought that in spite of his advice, his master must have called down a shower of treasure from the skies, and that they must have all died as a result. He proceeded down the road where he found his master's body. "Alas!" he cried, "he is dead because he did not heed my warning." Then he gathered sticks and made a fire on which he cremated his master's body.

Continuing down the road, he came upon the five hundred "Dispatchers," and further still he found the two hundred and fifty dead robbers. He saw that of the thousand men all but two had died. Feeling sure that there must be two survivors, and that these they probably fought as well, he pressed on to see where they had gone. Finally, he found the path they had taken into the jungle. There he found the treasure, with one robber lying dead with his rice bowl overturned at his side. Realizing the whole story at a glance, the Bodhisatta went to look for the missing man. At last found his body in the spot where it had been hidden. "And thus," the Bodhisatta thought, "because he would not follow my advice, my headstrong master destroyed himself and a thousand others. Truly, they that seek their own gain by mistaken and misguided means shall reap ruin, even as my master did." And he repeated this stanza:

> Misguided effort leads to loss, not gain.
> Thieves killed Vedabbha and then they were killed.

Thus spoke the Bodhisatta, and he went on to say, "And even as my master's misguided and misplaced effort in causing the rain of treasure to fall from heaven caused his own death and the destruction of others, every other man who tries to gain some advantage by foolish means will perish and involve others in his destruction."

The Bodhisatta's words rang throughout the forest while the tree fairies shouted applause. He carried the treasure off to his own home where he lived out his life giving alms and doing other good works. And when his life ended, he was reborn in a heavenly realm.

Then the Master said, "This is not the first time, brother, you were headstrong. You were headstrong in bygone times as well, and because of this you came to utter destruction." His lesson ended, he identified the birth by saying, "The headstrong monk was the Vedabbha-brahmin of those days, and I was his pupil."

49: Nakkatta Jātaka,
The Stars

Many Asian cultures practiced astrology, magic, and various occult rituals. But the Buddha was quite disparaging of these. His message was simple: wholesome actions have wholesome results, and unwholesome actions have unwholesome results. We live in a universe of causes and results, not magic. Nonetheless, as Buddhism moved into different Asian countries, many people who otherwise accepted the Buddha's teachings continued to believe in the occult.

It may seem like the poor bride in these stories is treated rather cavalierly. But a recent study determined that 55% of all marriages in the world are arranged, and that these marriages only have a 6% divorce rate. (Note that arranged marriages are not the same as forced marriages.) The people who are responsible for arranging the marriage are usually trying to find a good match, and the people in this story are from the same village. As a result, they probably knew each other well.

"The fool may watch." This story was told by the Master while at Jetavana. It is about a certain naked ascetic. Tradition says that a gentleman of the country near Sāvatthi asked for his son the hand in marriage of a young Sāvatthi lady of equal rank. After they arranged the day on which they would come to fetch the bride, he subsequently consulted a naked ascetic who was close with his family, as to whether the stars were favorable for holding the festivities that day.

"He didn't ask me before he arranged the day of the wedding," thought the indignant ascetic. "But having already arranged the day without consulting me, he is just making an empty gesture to me now. Very well. I will teach him a lesson."

So he said that the stars were not favorable for that day, that the wedding should not to be celebrated that day, and that if they were, great misfortune would come of it. So the country family, because of their faith in the ascetic, did not go for the bride that day.

But the bride's friends in the town had made all their preparations for celebrating the wedding, and when they saw that the other side did not show up, they said, "It was they who fixed the day, and yet they have not come, and we have gone to great expense to make the preparations. Who are these people? Let us marry the girl to someone else." So they found another bridegroom and gave the girl to him in marriage, going through with the festivities that they had prepared.

On the next day the country party came to get the bride. But the Sāvatthi people berated them, saying "You country folk are a bad lot. You chose the day yourselves, and then insulted us by not coming. We have given the girl to someone else." The country party started a fight, but in the end they went home the same way they came.

Now the monks learned about how that naked ascetic had sabotaged the festivity, and they began to talk about it in the Dharma Hall. Entering the hall, and learning about the subject of their conversation, the Master said, "Monks, this is not the first time that this same ascetic has sabotaged the festivities of that family. Out of annoyance with them, he did the same thing once before." And so saying, he told this story of the past.

Once upon a time when Brahmadatta was reigning in Benares, some townsfolk asked a country girl for her hand in marriage and had named the day for the wedding. Having already set the date of the wedding, they asked their family ascetic whether the stars were auspicious for the ceremony on that day. Irritated because they set the date without having first consulting him, the ascetic decided to ruin their marriage festivities for that day. Accordingly he said that the stars were not favorable for that day, and that if they persisted, grave misfortune would result. So in their faith in the ascetic, they stayed at home on the day of the wedding. When the country folk found that the town folk did not come, they said among themselves, "It was they who fixed the marriage for today, and now they have not come. Who are these people?" And they married the girl to someone else.

On the next day the townsfolk came and asked for the girl, but the country folk said, "You town people lack common decency. You named the day of the wedding, and yet you did not come to get the bride. So we married her to someone else."

"But we asked our ascetic, and he told us the stars were unfavorable. That's why we did not come, yesterday. Give us the girl."

"You didn't come at the proper time, and now she is another man's wife. How can we marry her twice over?"

49: Nakkatta Jātaka, The Stars

Figure: Nasty guru, bad astrologer

While they argued with one another, a wise man from the town came into the country on business. Hearing the townsfolk explain that they had consulted their ascetic and that their absence was due to the unfavorable disposition of the stars, he exclaimed, "What do the stars matter? Is it not a lucky thing to get the girl?" And, so saying, he repeated this stanza:

> *The fool may watch for "lucky days,"*
> *Yet luck will always miss.*
> *Luck itself is luck's own star.*
> *What can the stars achieve?*

As for the townsfolk, they did not get the girl for all their arguing and had to go off home again!

Then the Master said, "This is not the first time, monks, that this naked ascetic has ruined that family's festivities. He did just the same thing in bygone times as well." His lesson ended, he showed the connection and identified the birth by saying, "This ascetic was also the ascetic of those days, and the families too were the same. I myself was the wise and good man who uttered the stanza."

50: Dummedha Jātaka,
The Evildoers

In this story the Bodhisatta becomes the King. He uses his authority to end the practice of animal sacrifice and to force his subjects to follow the Five Precepts. This may seem a little heavy-handed, but maybe it is not really such a bad idea. Imagine laws that promote good behavior.

"A thousand evildoers." This story was told by the Master while at Jetavana. It is about actions done for the world's good, as will be explained in the Twelfth Book in the Mahā Kaṇha Jātaka (*Jātaka 469*).

Once upon a time when Brahmadatta was reigning in Benares, the Bodhisatta was reborn in the womb of the Queen Consort. When he was born, he was named Prince Brahmadatta on his naming day. By the time he was sixteen years of age, he had been well educated at Takkasilā University, he had learned the Three Vedas by heart, and he was versed in the Eighteen Branches of Knowledge (*also called the 18 vidhyasthanams*). And his father made him a minister in the government.

Now in those days the Benares folk were enamored of festivals to gods, and they used to show honor to gods. It was their practice to sacrifice many sheep, goats, poultry, swine, and living creatures, and to perform their rituals not merely with flowers and perfumes but with gory carcasses. The future Lord of Mercy thought to himself, "These people are led astray by superstition. Men cruelly sacrifice life. They are given up to paganism. But when I become King at my father's death, I will end this destruction of life. I will devise some clever scheme whereby the evil will be stopped without harming a single human being."

With this in mind, the prince mounted his chariot one day and drove out of the city. On the way he saw a crowd gathered at a holy banyan tree. There was a fairy who had been reborn in that tree, and they were praying to the fairy to grant them sons and daughters and honor and wealth. Descending from his chariot, the Bodhisatta went over to the tree and acted like a worshipper. He made offerings of perfumes and flowers, sprinkled the tree with water, and circumambulated its trunk. Then mounting his chariot again, he went back into the city.

Thereafter the prince made similar journeys to the tree, and he worshipped it like a true believer in gods.

In due course, when his father died, the Bodhisatta ascended to the throne. Shunning the four evil courses (*desire, aversion, delusion, and fear*), and practicing the ten royal virtues (*generosity, morality, renunciation, honesty, gentleness, asceticism, non-violence, patience, uprightness*), he ruled his people in righteousness. And now that he was King, the Bodhisatta determined to fulfill his vow. So he called together his ministers, the brahmins, the nobility, and the other orders of the people, and he asked them whether they knew how he had become King. But no one could tell him.

"Have you ever seen me reverently worshipping a banyan tree with perfumes and the like, and bowing down before it?"

"Sire, we have," they answered.

"When I did this, I was making a vow. The vow was that if I ever became King, I would offer a sacrifice to that tree. And now that I have come to be King with the help of that god, I will make my promised sacrifice. So prepare it with all speed."

"But what are we to sacrifice?" they asked.

"My vow," said the King, "was this. I will sacrifice all who are addicted to the Five Sins (*breaking the Five Precepts*), which includes the slaughter of living creatures, and all who walk in the Ten Paths of Unrighteousness (*killing, stealing, sexual misconduct, lying, malicious speech, harsh speech, idle chatter, covetousness, ill will, and wrong view*). Then I will make my offering with their flesh and their blood and with their entrails and their vital organs. So proclaim by the beat of the drum that our lord the King in his days as prince vowed that if he ever became King, he would execute and offer up as a sacrifice all of his subjects who break the Precepts. And now the King will execute 1,000 of those who are addicted to the Five Sins or walk in the Ten Paths of Unrighteousness. I will make a sacrifice with the hearts and the flesh of the 1,000 in the god's honor. Proclaim this so that everyone will know it throughout the city. Anyone who violates this decree after today," added the King, "will be executed and offered as a sacrifice to the god in fulfillment of my vow." And to make his meaning clear the King uttered this stanza:

50: Dummedha Jātaka, The Evildoers

I once vowed to execute 1,000 evildoers
In pious gratitude.
And there are so many evildoers,
That I can now fulfill my vow.

Figure: Sacrifice Animals at Your Own Risk

Obedient to the King's commands, the ministers proclaimed the decree by the beat of the drum throughout the length and breadth of Benares. Such was the effect of the proclamation on the townsfolk that not a single person persisted in the old wickedness. And throughout the Bodhisatta's reign not a single man was convicted of breaking the decree. Thus, without harming a single one of his subjects, the Bodhisatta made them observe the Precepts. And at the close of a life of generosity and other good works, he passed away with his followers to inhabit the city of the devas.

The Master said, "This is not the first time, monks, that the Buddha has acted for the world's good. He acted in the same way in bygone times as well." His lesson ended, he showed the connection and identified the birth by saying, "The Buddha's disciples were the ministers of those days, and I myself was the King of Benares."

CPSIA information can be obtained
at www.ICGtesting.com
Printed in the USA
LVHW051621250121
677444LV00044B/2580